Speeches On The Road
To The White House

FOR REFERENCE

NOT TO BE TAKEN FROM THIS ROOM

MAUREEN HARRISON & STEVE GILBERT
EDITORS

EXCELLENT BOOKS
CARLSBAD, CALIFORNIA

EXCELLENT BOOKS
Post Office Box 131322
Carlsbad, CA 92013-1322

Publisher's Cataloging in Publication Data

Barack Obama: Speeches On The Road To The White House/
    Maureen Harrison, Steve Gilbert, editors.
        p.   cm.
    Bibliography: p.
    1. Obama, Barack, 1961–
    I. Title. II. Harrison, Maureen. III. Gilbert, Steve.
    PN6121 2009   LC 2008908015
    808.85 O16 2009
    ISBN 978-1-880780-30-5

INTRODUCTION

There is no eloquence without a man behind it.
—Ralph Waldo Emerson

Barack Obama: Speeches On The Road To The White House is a wide-ranging and representative collection of thirty major speeches by Barack Obama edited down to their eloquent essentials.

Presented in a straightforward chronological format, in which each speech is offered in its contemporary context, this comprehensive collection of these most important and thought-provoking speeches traces the evolution of Barack Obama's use of powerfully persuasive political language over a period of six tumultuous years—beginning with 2002's anti-Iraq "Dumb Wars Speech" and culminating with the thrilling Election Night 2008 "Victory Speech."

Eloquent in their delivery and inspiring in their content, the speeches in *Barack Obama: Speeches On The Road To The White House* will inform readers, writers, and researchers. The extraordinary speeches—2004's *We Are One People,* 2006's *This Is Our Time* and 2008's *Yes, We Can!*—shattered the political sound-bite barrier and powered Barack Obama's historic campaign for the American Presidency.

Of special interest to all Americans, black and white, is Barack Obama's 2008 speech, *A More Perfect Union,* known more commonly as "The Race Speech," in which the first African-American presidential nominee confronts the question of race: *I have asserted a firm conviction—a conviction rooted in my faith in God and my faith in the American people—that working together we can move beyond some of our old racial wounds, and that in fact we have no choice if we are to continue on the path of a more perfect union.*

Barack Obama: Speeches On The Road To The White House is designed to be an easy-to-access, all-in one anthology of the historic speeches that changed American politics forever.

Only in America could a tall, skinny Midwestern politician, little known outside his adopted Illinois, be invited to speak before an important political gathering and, as a result of one passionately eloquent speech, become a Presidential contender overnight.

This could be the improbable plot of one of Horatio Alger's nineteenth century "rags-to-riches" dime novels. Yet, in the nineteenth century—on February 27, 1860, to be exact—such a politician, Abraham Lincoln, was invited to speak at the Cooper Union Institute in New York. This important political gathering placed him on the road to the White House. Lincoln told that long-ago audience: *Let us have faith that Right makes Might, and in that faith, let us, to the end, dare to do our duty as we understand it.*

In the Pulitzer Prize-winning history, *Lincoln at Cooper Union: The Speech That Made Abraham Lincoln President*, Harold Holzer writes, "It is fair to say that never before or since in American history has a single speech so dramatically catapulted a candidate toward the White House."

That was true until the present day, when another single speech by a tall, skinny Midwestern politician, little known outside his adopted Illinois, was delivered with eloquence and passion, and placed Barack Obama on the road to the White House. *We are one people*, Obama told the 2004 National Democratic Convention, *all of us pledging allegiance to the stars and stripes, all of us defending the United States of America. In the end, that's what this election is about. Do we participate in a politics of cynicism or do we participate in a politics of hope?*

The common message in all thirty speeches contained in *Barack Obama: Speeches On The Road To The White House* is about "the politics of hope." We hope that readers and researchers alike find in this book insight into the man behind that message.

—M.H. & S.G.

TABLE OF SPEECHES

CHOOSING OUR BETTER HISTORY
The Time for Change Speech

We can choose hope over fear, unity over division, the promise of change over the power of the status quo.... We can come together as one nation, and one people, and once more choose our better history.

—October 29, 2008

YES, WE CAN!
The Victory Speech

This is our time ... to reclaim the American dream and reaffirm that fundamental truth that, out of many, we are one, that while we breathe, we hope. And, where we are met with cynicism and doubts and those who tell us that we can't, we will respond with that timeless creed that sums up the spirit of a people—Yes, we can!

—November 4, 2008

BIBLIOGRAPHY

To Ben Parsons, Who Told Us So

DUMB WARS
An Anti-Iraq War Speech
October 26, 2002

(Chicago, Illinois) Barack Obama delivered this speech to an anti-war rally in Chicago's Federal Plaza, taking for his theme his opposition, not to all wars but, to the imminent Iraq War: *I am not opposed to all wars. I'm opposed to dumb wars. So for those of us who seek a more just and secure world for our children, let us send a clear message to the President.*

I stand before you as someone who is not opposed to war in all circumstances. The Civil War was one of the bloodiest in history, and yet it was only through the crucible of the sword, the sacrifice of multitudes, that we could begin to perfect this union and drive the scourge of slavery from our soil.

I don't oppose all wars. My grandfather signed up for a war the day after Pearl Harbor was bombed, fought in Patton's army. He fought in the name of a larger freedom, part of that arsenal of democracy that triumphed over evil.

I don't oppose all wars. After September 11, after witnessing the carnage and destruction, the dust and the tears, I supported this administration's pledge to hunt down and root out those who would slaughter innocents in the name of intolerance, and I would willingly take up arms myself to prevent such tragedy from happening again.

I don't oppose all wars. What I am opposed to is a dumb war. What I am opposed to is a rash war. What I am opposed to is the cynical attempt by … armchair weekend warriors in this administration to shove their own ideological agendas down our throats, irrespective of the costs in lives lost and in hardships borne. What I am opposed to is the attempt by political hacks … to distract us from a rise in the uninsured, a rise in the poverty rate, a drop in the median income, to distract us from corporate scandals and a stock market that has just gone through the worst month since the Great Depression.

That's what I'm opposed to. A dumb war. A rash war. A war based not on reason but on passion, not on principle but on politics.

Now let me be clear: I suffer no illusions about Saddam Hussein. He is a brutal man. A ruthless man. A man who butchers his own people to secure his own power. The world, and the Iraqi people, would be better off without him. But I also know that Saddam poses no imminent and direct threat to the United States, or to his neighbors and that in concert with the international community he can be contained until, in the way of all petty dictators, he falls away into the dustbin of history.

I know that even a successful war against Iraq will require a U.S. occupation of undetermined length, at undetermined cost, with undetermined consequences. I know that an invasion of Iraq without a clear rationale and without strong international support will only fan the flames of the Middle East, and encourage the worst, rather than best, impulses of the Arab world, and strengthen the recruitment arm of al-Qaeda.

I am not opposed to all wars. I'm opposed to dumb wars. So for those of us who seek a more just and secure world for our children, let us send a clear message to the President.

You want a fight, President Bush? Let's finish the fight with Bin Laden and al-Qaeda, through effective, coordinated intelligence, and a shutting down of the financial networks that support terrorism, and a homeland security program that involves more than color-coded warnings.

You want a fight, President Bush? Let's fight to make sure that…we vigorously enforce a nonproliferation treaty, and that former enemies and current allies like Russia safeguard and ultimately eliminate their stores of nuclear material, and that nations like Pakistan and India never use the terrible weapons already in their possession, and that the arms merchants in our own country stop feeding the countless wars that rage across the globe.

You want a fight, President Bush? Let's fight to make sure our so-called allies in the Middle East, the Saudis and the Egyptians, stop oppressing their own people, and suppressing dissent, and tolerating corruption and inequality, and mismanaging their economies so that their youth grow up without education, without prospects, without hope, the ready recruits of terrorist cells.

You want a fight, President Bush? Let's fight to wean ourselves off Middle East oil through an energy policy that doesn't simply serve the interests of Exxon and Mobil.

Those are the battles that we need to fight. Those are the battles that we willingly join. The battles against ignorance and intolerance. Corruption and greed. Poverty and despair.

WE ARE ONE PEOPLE!
Keynote Address
To The Democratic National Convention
July 28, 2004

(Boston, Massachusetts) Barack Obama delivered the keynote speech at the 2004 Democratic National Convention, taking for his theme national unity: *We are one people, all of us pledging allegiance to the stars and stripes, all of us defending the United States of America. In the end, that's what this election is about. Do we participate in a politics of cynicism or do we participate in a politics of hope?*

On behalf of the great state of Illinois, crossroads of a nation, land of Lincoln, let me express my deepest gratitude for the privilege of addressing this convention. Tonight is a particular honor for me because, let's face it, my presence on this stage is pretty unlikely. My father was a foreign student, born and raised in a small village in Kenya. He grew up herding goats, went to school in a tin-roof shack. His father, my grandfather, was a cook, a domestic servant to the British.

But my grandfather had larger dreams for his son. Through hard work and perseverance my father got a scholarship to study in a magical place, America, that stood as a beacon of freedom and opportunity to so many who had come before.

While studying here, my father met my mother. She was born in a town on the other side of the world, in Kansas.

Her father worked on oil rigs and farms through most of the Depression. The day after Pearl Harbor my grandfather signed up for duty, joined Patton's army and marched across Europe. Back home, my grandmother raised their baby and went to work on a bomber assembly line. After the war, they studied on the GI Bill, bought a house through FHA, and moved west, all the way to Hawaii, in search of opportunity.

And they, too, had big dreams for their daughter, a common dream, born of two continents.

My parents shared not only an improbable love; they shared an abiding faith in the possibilities of this nation. They would give me an African name, Barack, or "blessed," believing that in a tolerant America your name is no barrier to success.

They imagined me going to the best schools in the land, even though they weren't rich, because in a generous America you don't have to be rich to achieve your potential.

They're both passed away now. And yet, I know that, on this night, they look down on me with pride.

And I stand here today, grateful for the diversity of my heritage, aware that my parents' dreams live on in my two precious daughters.

I stand here knowing that my story is part of the larger American story, that I owe a debt to all of those who came before me, and that, in no other country on Earth, is my story even possible.

Tonight, we gather to affirm the greatness of our nation, not because of the height of our skyscrapers, or the power of our military, or the size of our economy. Our pride is based on a very simple premise, summed up in a declaration made over two hundred years ago,

> "We hold these truths to be self-evident, that all men are created equal. That they are endowed by their Creator with certain inalienable rights. That among these are life, liberty and the pursuit of happiness."

That is the true genius of America, a faith in the simple dreams, an insistence on small miracles. That we can tuck in our children at night and know they are fed and clothed and safe from harm. That we can say what we think, write what we think, without hearing a sudden knock on the door. That we can have an idea and start our own business without paying a bribe. That we can participate in the political process without fear of retribution, and that our votes will be counted—or at least, most of the time.

This year, in this election, we are called to reaffirm our values and commitments, to hold them against a hard reality and see how we are measuring up to the legacy of our forbearers and the promise of future generations.

And fellow Americans—Democrats, Republicans, Independents—I say to you tonight: we have more work to do. More work to do for the workers I met in Galesburg, Illinois, who are losing their union jobs at the Maytag plant that's moving to Mexico, and now are having to compete with their own children for jobs that pay seven bucks an hour. More to do for the father I met who was losing his job and choking back tears, wondering how he would pay $4,500 a month for the drugs his son needs without the health benefits that he counted on. More to do for the young woman in East St. Louis, and thousands more like her, who has the grades, has the drive, has the will, but doesn't have the money to go to college.

Now don't get me wrong. The people I meet in small towns and big cities, in diners and office parks, they don't expect government to solve all their problems. They know they have to work hard to get ahead and they want to.

Go into the collar counties around Chicago, and people will tell you they don't want their tax money wasted by a welfare agency or the Pentagon.

Go into any inner city neighborhood, and folks will tell you that government alone can't teach our kids to learn. They know that parents have to parent, that children can't achieve unless we raise their expectations and turn off the television sets and eradicate the slander that says a black youth with a book is acting white. They know those things.

People don't expect government to solve all their problems. But they sense, deep in their bones, that with just a change in priorities, we can make sure that every child in America has a decent shot at life, and that the doors of opportunity remain open to all. They know we can do better. And they want that choice.

.... You know, a while back, I met a young man named Shamus at the VFW Hall in East Moline, Illinois. He was a good-looking kid, 6-2 or 6-3, clear-eyed, with an easy smile. He told me he'd joined the Marines and was heading to Iraq the following week.

And as I listened to him explain why he'd enlisted, his absolute faith in our country and its leaders, his devotion to duty and service, I thought this young man was all that any of us might hope for in a child. But then I asked myself: Are we serving Shamus as well as he was serving us?

I thought of the 900 men and women, sons and daughters, husbands and wives, friends and neighbors, who will not be returning to their hometowns. I thought of families I had met who were struggling to get by without a loved one's full income, or whose loved ones had returned with a limb missing or nerves shattered, but who still lacked long-term health benefits because they were reservists.

When we send our young men and women into harm's way, we have a solemn obligation not to fudge the numbers or shade the truth about why they're going, to care for their families while they're gone, to tend to the soldiers upon their return, and to never ever go to war without enough troops to win the war, secure the peace, and earn the respect of the world.

Now let me be clear. Let me be clear. We have real enemies in the world. These enemies must be found. They must be pursued and they must be defeated.

…. And … it's not enough for just some of us to prosper. For alongside our famous individualism, there's another ingredient in the American saga. A belief that we are all connected as one people.

If there's a child on the South Side of Chicago who can't read, that matters to me, even if it's not my child.

If there's a senior citizen somewhere who can't pay for their prescription and has to choose between medicine and the rent, that makes my life poorer, even if it's not my grandparent.

If there's an Arab-American family being rounded up without benefit of an attorney or due process, that threatens my civil liberties.

It is that fundamental belief—it is that fundamental belief—I am my brother's keeper, I am my sister's keeper—that makes this country work.

It's what allows us to pursue our individual dreams, yet still come together as a single American family. "E pluribus unum." Out of many, one.

Now even as we speak, there are those who are preparing to divide us, the spin masters and negative ad peddlers who embrace the politics of anything goes.

Well, I say to them tonight, there's not a liberal America and a conservative America—there is the United States of America.

There's not a black America and white America and Latino America and Asian America—there is the United States of America.

The pundits, the pundits like to slice and dice our country into red states and blue states—red states for Republicans, blue states for Democrats. But I've got news for them, too. We worship an awesome God in the blue states, and we don't like federal agents poking around our libraries in the red states.

We coach Little League in the blue states and have gay friends in the red states.

There are patriots who opposed the war in Iraq and patriots who supported it.

We are one people, all of us pledging allegiance to the stars and stripes, all of us defending the United States of America.

In the end, that's what this election is about. Do we participate in a politics of cynicism or do we participate in a politics of hope?

.... I'm not talking about blind optimism here—the almost willful ignorance that thinks unemployment will go away if we just don't talk about it, or the health care crisis will solve itself if we just ignore it.

That's not what I'm talking about. I'm talking about something more substantial. It's the hope of slaves sitting around a fire singing freedom songs; the hope of immigrants setting out for distant shores; the hope of a young naval lieutenant bravely patrolling the Mekong Delta; the hope of a mill worker's son who dares to defy the odds; the hope of a skinny kid with a funny name who believes that America has a place for him, too.

Hope in the face of difficulty, hope in the face of uncertainty, the audacity of hope.

In the end, that is God's greatest gift to us, the bedrock of this nation; a belief in things not seen; a belief that there are better days ahead.

I believe we can give our middle class relief and provide working families with a road to opportunity.

I believe we can provide jobs to the jobless, homes to the homeless, and reclaim young people in cities across America from violence and despair.

I believe that we have a righteous wind at our backs, and that as we stand on the crossroads of history, we can make the right choices and meet the challenges that face us.

America, tonight, if you feel the same energy that I do, if you feel the same urgency that I do, if you feel the same passion that I do, if you feel the same hopefulness that I do, if we do what we must do, then I have no doubt that all across the country, from Florida to Oregon, from Washington to Maine, the people will rise up in November, and … this country will reclaim its promise. And out of this long political darkness a brighter day will come.

Thank you very much, everybody. God bless you.

SAVING SOCIAL SECURITY
A Speech At The National Press Club
April 26, 2005

(Washington, D.C.) Barack Obama delivered this speech at the National Press Club, taking as his theme the saving of Social Security: *These are important questions that require us to work together, not in a manufactured panic about a genuine but solvable problem, but with the spirit of pragmatism and innovation that will offer every American the secure retirement they have earned.*

Thank you. It's great to be here at the National Press Club....

By the time the Senate Finance Committee holds the first Senate hearing on the President's Social Security plan today, we'll have heard just about everything there is to be said about the issue. We've heard about privatization and benefit cuts, about massive new debt and huge new risks, and we've even been scared into thinking the system will go broke when our kids retire, even though we know there'll be enough money then to pay the vast majority of benefits.... But aside from the usual back and forth of this debate, I can't help but think about the larger issue at stake here.

Think about the America that Franklin Roosevelt saw when he looked out the windows of the White House from his wheelchair—an America where too many were ill-fed, ill-clothed, ill-housed, and insecure. An America where more and more Americans were finding themselves on the losing end of a new economy, and where there was nothing available to cushion their fall.

Some thought that our country didn't have a responsibility to do anything about these problems, that people would be better off left to their own devices and the whims of the market. Others believed that American capitalism had failed and that it was time to try something else altogether.

But our President believed deeply in the American idea.

He understood that the freedom to pursue our own individual dreams is made possible by the promise that if fate causes us to stumble or fall, our larger American family will be there to lift us up. That if we're willing to share even a small amount of life's risks and rewards with each other, then we'll all have the chance to make the most of our God-given potential.

And because Franklin Roosevelt had the courage to act on this idea, individual Americans were able to get back on their feet and build a shared prosperity that is still the envy of the world.

The New Deal gave the laid-off worker a guarantee that he could count on unemployment insurance to put food on his family's table while he looked for a new job. It gave the young man who suffered a debilitating accident assurance that he could count on disability benefits to get him through the tough times. A widow might still raise her children without the indignity of charity. And Franklin Roosevelt's greatest legacy promised the couple who put in a lifetime of sacrifice and hard work that they could retire in comfort and dignity because of Social Security.

Today, we're told by those who want to privatize that promise how much things are different and times have changed since Roosevelt's day.

I couldn't agree more.

A child born in this new century is likely to start his life with both parents—or a single parent—working full-time jobs. They'll try their hardest to juggle work and family, but they'll end up needing child care to keep him safe, cared for, and educated early.

They'll want to give him the best education possible, but unless they live in a wealthy town with good public schools, they'll have to settle for less or find the money for private schools.

This student will study hard and dream of going to the best colleges in the country, but with tuition rising higher and faster than ever before, he may have to postpone those dreams or start life deeper in debt than any generation before him.

When he graduates from college, this young man will find a job market where middle-class manufacturing jobs with good benefits have long been replaced with low-wage, low-benefit service sector jobs and high-skill, high-wage jobs of the future.

To get those good jobs, he'll need the skills and knowledge to not only compete with other workers in America, but with highly skilled and highly knowledgeable workers all over the world who are being recruited by the same companies that once made their home in this country.

When he finally starts his job, he'll want health insurance, but rising costs mean that fewer employers can afford to provide that benefit, and when they do, fewer employees can afford the record premiums.

When he starts a family, he'll want to buy a house and a car and pay for child care and college for his own children, but as he watches the lucky few benefit from lucrative bonuses and tax shelters, he'll see his own tax burden rise and his own paycheck barely cover this month's bills.

And when he retires, he'll hope that he and his wife have saved enough, but if there wasn't enough to save, he'll hope that there will still be two Social Security checks that come to the house every month.

These are the challenges we face at the beginning of the 21st Century. We shouldn't exaggerate; we aren't seeing the absolute deprivation of the Great Depression. But it cannot be denied that families face more risk and greater insecurity than we have known since FDR's time, even as those families have fewer resources available to help pull themselves through the tough spots.

Whereas people were once able to count on their employer to provide health care, pensions, and a job that would last a lifetime, today's worker wonders if suffering a heart attack will cause his employer to drop his coverage, worries about how much he can contribute to his own pension fund, and fears the possibility that he might walk into work tomorrow and find his job outsourced.

Yet, just as the naysayers in Roosevelt's day told us that there was nothing we could do to help people help themselves, the people in power today are telling us that instead of sharing the risks of the new economy, we should shoulder them on our own.

In the end, this is what the debate over the future of Social Security is truly about.

After a lifetime of hard work and contribution to this country, do we tell our seniors that they're on their own, or that we're here for them to provide a basic standard of living? Is the dignity of life in their latter years their problem, or one we all share?

Since this is Washington, you won't hear them answer those questions directly when they talk about Social Security. Instead, they use the word "reform" when they mean "privatize," and they use "strengthen" when they really mean "dismantle." They tell us there's a crisis to get us all riled up so we'll sit down and listen to their plan to privatize.

But we know what the whole thing's really about.

It's not just about cutting guaranteed benefits by up to fifty percent—though it certainly does that.

It's not just about borrowing $5 trillion from countries like China and Japan to finance the plan—after all, we know how fiscal conservatives hate debt and deficit.

And it's not even about the ability of private accounts to finance the gap in the system—because even the privatization advocates admit they don't.

What this whole thing is about, and why conservatives have been pushing it so hard for so long now, is summed up in one sentence in one White House memo that somehow made its way out of the White House: "For the first time in six decades, the Social Security battle is one we can win—and in doing so, we can help transform the political and philosophical landscape of the country."

And there it is. Since Social Security was first signed into law almost seventy years ago, at a time when FDR's opponents were calling it a hoax that would never work and some likened it to communism, there has been movement after movement to get rid of the program for purely ideological reasons. Because some still believe that we can't solve the problems we face as one American community; they think this country works better when we're left to face fate by ourselves.

I understand this view. There's something bracing about the Social Darwinist idea, the idea that there isn't a problem that the unfettered free market can't solve. It requires no sacrifice on the part of those of us who have won life's lottery—and doesn't consider who our parents were, or the education we received, or the right breaks that came at the right time.

But I couldn't disagree more. If we privatize Social Security, what will we tell retirees whose investments in the stock market went badly? We're sorry? Keep working? You're on your own?

When people's expected benefits get cut and they have to choose between their groceries and their prescriptions, what will we say then? That's not our problem?

When our debt climbs so high that our children face sky-high taxes just as they're starting their first job, what will we tell them? Deal with it yourselves?

This isn't how America works. This isn't how we saved millions of seniors from a life of poverty seventy years ago. This isn't how we sent a greatest generation of veterans to college so they could build the greatest middle-class in history. And this isn't how we should face the challenges of this new century either.

And yet, this is the direction they're trying to take America on almost every issue. Instead of trying to contain the skyrocketing cost of health care and expand access to the uninsured, the idea behind the President's Health Savings Accounts are to leave the system alone and give you a few extra bucks to go find a plan you can afford on your own. You deal with double digit inflation by going to the doctor less. Instead of strengthening a pension system that provides defined benefits to employees who've worked a lifetime, we'll give you a tax break and hope that you invest well and save well in your own little account. And if none of this works—if you couldn't find affordable insurance and suffer an illness that leaves you thousands of dollars in debt—then you should no longer count on being able to start over by declaring bankruptcy because they've changed the law to put the burden of debt squarely on your shoulders.

Taking responsibility for oneself and showing individual initiative are American values we all share. Frankly, they're values we could stand to see more of in a culture where the buck is too often passed to the next guy. They are values we could use more of here in Washington too.

But the irony of this all-out assault against every existing form of social insurance is that these safety nets are exactly what encourage each of us to be risk-takers and entrepreneurs who are free to pursue our individual ambitions. We get into a car knowing that if someone rear-ends us, they will have insurance to pay for the repairs. We buy a house knowing that our investment is protected by homeowners insurance. We take a chance on start-ups and small businesses because we know that if they fail, there are protections available to cushion our fall. Corporations across America have limited liability for this very reason. Families should too—and that's why we need social insurance. This is how the market works.

This is how America works. And if we want it to keep working, we need to develop new ways for all of us to share the new risks of a 21st Century economy, not destroy what we already have.

The genius of Roosevelt was putting into practice the idea that America doesn't have to be a place where our individual aspirations are at war with our common good; it's a place where one makes the other possible.

I think we will save Social Security from privatization this year. And in doing so, we will affirm our belief that we are all connected as one people—ready to share life's risks and rewards for the benefit of each and the good of all.

Let me close by suggesting that Democrats are absolutely united in the need to strengthen Social Security and make it solvent for future generations. We know that, and we want that. And I believe that both Democrats and Republicans can work together to do that. While we're at it, we can begin a debate about the real challenges America faces as the baby boomers begin to retire.

About getting a handle on the growing cost of health care and prescription drugs. About increasing individual and national savings. About strengthening our pension system for the 21st Century.

These are important questions that require us to work together, not in a manufactured panic about a genuine but solvable problem, but with the spirit of pragmatism and innovation that will offer every American the secure retirement they have earned.

You know, there are times in the life of this nation where we are individual citizens going about our own business, enjoying the freedoms we've been blessed with.

And then there are times when we are one America, linked by the dignity of each and the destiny of all.

The debate over the future of Social Security must be one of these times.

The people I've met since starting my campaign tell me they don't want a big government that's running their lives, but they do want an active government that will give them the opportunity to make the most of their lives.

Starting with the child born today and the senior moving into the twilight of life, together we can provide that opportunity.

The day Franklin Roosevelt signed the Social Security Act of 1935 into law, he began by saying that "Today, a hope of many years' standing is in large part fulfilled."

It is now time to fulfill our hope for an America where we're in this together—for our seniors, for our children, and for every American in the years and generations yet to come.

THE COURAGE TO DO EXTRAORDINARY THINGS
A Speech To The NAACP's
Fight for Freedom Fund
May 2, 2005

(Detroit, Michigan) Barack Obama delivered this speech to the NAACP Fight for Freedom Fund Dinner, taking as his theme individual responsibility: *In America, ordinary citizens can somehow find in their hearts the courage to do extraordinary things. That change is never easy, but always possible. And it comes not from violence or militancy or the kind of politics that pits us against each other and plays on our worst fears, but from great discipline and organization, and from a strong message of hope.*

Thank you. Half a century after the first few hundred people sat for justice and equality at these tables, I am honored to be here with this crowd of thousands at the 50th NAACP Fight for Freedom Fund Dinner.

Founded at a time when we were constantly reminded how the world around us was separate and unequal—when the idea of legal rights for black folks was almost a contradiction in terms—when lunch counters and bus seats and water fountains were luxuries you had to fight for and march for, the 50th anniversary of the Fight for Freedom Dinner reminds us of just how far our struggle has come.

I was reminded of this last month, when I had the honor of going to Atlanta to speak at John Lewis's 65th birthday celebration. Many of the luminaries of the Civil Rights Movement were down there, and I had the great honor of sitting between Ethel Kennedy and Coretta Scott King, who both turned to me and said "we're really looking forward to hearing you speak." Now that's a really intimidating thing!

And as I stood up there next to John Lewis—not a giant in stature, but a giant of compassion and courage—I thought to myself, never in a million years would I have guessed that I'd be serving in Congress with John Lewis.

And then I thought, you know, there was once a time when John Lewis might never have guessed that he'd be serving in Congress.

And there was a time not long before that when people might never have guessed that someday black folks would be able to go to the polls, pick up a ballot, make their voice heard, and elect that Congress.

But we can, and many of us are here, because people like John Lewis believed. Because people feared nothing and risked everything for those beliefs. Because they saw injustice and endured pain in order to right what was wrong. We're here tonight because of them, and to them we owe the deepest gratitude.

The road we have taken to this point has not been easy. But, then again, the road to change never is.

Some of you might know that I taught Constitutional Law at the Chicago Law School for awhile. And one of the courses I taught was a course in race and law, where we chronicled the history of race in this country and people's struggle to achieve freedom in the courts and on the streets. And often times my students would come up to me and say things like,

"Boy, I wish I could've been around at the height of the Civil Rights Movement. Because things seemed so clear at the time. And while there may have been room for debate on some things, the clarity of the cause and the need for the movement were crystal clear, and you didn't have the ambiguities you have today.

"Because it's one thing to know that everyone has a seat at the lunch counter, but how do we figure out how everyone can pay for the meal? It was easy to figure out that blacks and whites should be able to go to school together, but how do we make sure that every child is equipped and ready to graduate? It was easy to talk about dogs and fire hoses, but how do we talk about getting drugs and guns off the streets?"

This is what they told me.

And of course, I reminded them that it wasn't very easy at all. That the moral certainties we now take for granted—that separate can never be equal, that the blessings of liberty enshrined in our Constitution belong to all of us, that our children should be able to go to school together and play together and grow up together—were anything but certain in 1965.

I reminded them that even within the African-American community, there was disagreement about how much to stir things up. We have a church in Chicago that's on what used to be known as State Park Way. After Dr. King's assassination, the street was renamed to Martin Luther King Jr. Drive. But the pastor of the church—a prominent African-American in the community—hated Dr. King so bad that he actually changed the address of the church.

And so it's never been clear. And it's never been easy. To get to where we are today, it took struggle and sacrifice, discipline and tremendous courage.

And sometimes, when I reflect on those giants of the Civil Rights movement, I wonder—where did you find that courage? John Lewis, where did you find that courage? Dorothy Height, where did you find that courage? Rosa Parks, where did you find that courage?

When you're facing row after row of state troopers on horseback armed with billy clubs and tear gas—when they're coming toward you spewing hatred and violence—how do you simply stop, kneel down, and pray to the Lord for salvation?

Where do you find that courage?

I don't know. But I do know that it's worth examining because the challenges we face today are going to require this kind of courage. The battle lines may have shifted and the barriers to equality may be new, but what's not new is the need for everyday heroes to stand up and speak out for what they believe is right.

Fifty years ago this country decided that Linda Brown shouldn't have to walk miles and miles to school every morning when there was a white school just four blocks away because when it comes to education in America, separate can never be equal.

Now that ruling came about because the NAACP was willing to fight tirelessly and risk its reputation; because everyday Americans—black and white—were willing to take to the streets and risk their freedom. Because people showed courage.

Fifty years later, what kind of courage are we showing to ensure that our schools are foundations of opportunity for our children? In a world where kids from Detroit aren't just competing with kids from Macomb for middle-class jobs, but with kids from Malaysia and New Delhi, ensuring that every American child gets the best education possible is the new civil rights challenge of our time.

A student today armed with only a high school diploma will earn an average of only $25,000 a year—if you're African-American, it's fourteen percent less than that. Meanwhile, countries like China are graduating twice as many students with a college degree as we do. We're falling behind, and if want our kids to have the same chances we had in life, we must work harder to catch up.

So what are we doing about it?

When we see that America has one of the highest high school dropout rates in the industrialized world—even higher for African-Americans and Hispanics, what are we doing about it?

When we see that our high school seniors are scoring lower on their math and science tests than almost any other students in the world at a time when expertise in these areas is the ticket to a high-wage job, what are we doing about it?

When we see that for every hundred students who enter ninth grade, only eighteen—eighteen—will earn any kind of college degree within six years of graduating high school, what are we doing about it?

And when we see broken schools, old textbooks, and classrooms bursting at the seams, what are we doing about that?

I'll tell you what they've been doing in Washington. In Washington, they'll talk about the importance of education one day and sign big tax cuts that starve our schools the next. They'll talk about Leaving No Child Behind but then say nothing when it becomes obvious that they've left the money behind. In the budget they passed this week in Congress, they gave out over $100 billion in tax cuts, on top of the trillions they've already given to the wealthiest few and most profitable corporations.

One hundred billion dollars. Think about what that could do for our kids if we invested that in our schools. Think of how many new schools we could build, how many great teachers we could recruit, what kind of computers and technology we could put in our classrooms. Think about how much we could invest in math and science so our kids could be prepared for the 21st Century economy. Think about how many kids we could send to college who've worked hard, studied hard, but just can't afford the tuition.

Think about all that potential and all that opportunity. Think about the choice Washington made instead. And now think about what you can do about it.

I believe we have a mutual responsibility to make sure our schools are properly funded, our teachers are properly paid, and our students have access to an affordable college education. And if we don't do something about all that, than nothing else matters.

But I also believe we have an individual responsibility as well.

Our grandparents used to tell us that being Black means you have to work twice as hard to succeed in life. And so I ask today, can we honestly say our kids are working twice as hard as the kids in India and China who are graduating ahead of us, with better test scores and the tools they need to kick our butts on the job market? Can we honestly say our teachers are working twice as hard, or our parents?

One thing's for sure, I certainly know that Washington's not working twice as hard—and that's something each of us has a role in changing. Because if we want change in our education system—if we want our schools to be less crowded and funded more equitably; if we want our children to take the courses that will get them ready for the 21st Century; if we want our teachers to be paid what they're worth and armed with the tools they need to prepare our kids—then we need to summon the same courage today that those giants of the Civil Rights movement summoned half a century ago.

Because more than anything else, these anniversaries—of the Voting Rights Act and the Civil Rights Act and the Fight for Freedom Fund Dinner—they remind us that in America, ordinary citizens can somehow find in their hearts the courage to do extraordinary things. That change is never easy, but always possible. And it comes not from violence or militancy or the kind of politics that pits us against each other and plays on our worst fears, but from great discipline and organization, and from a strong message of hope.

And when we look at these challenges and think, how can we do this? How can we cut through the apathy and the partisanship and the business-as-usual culture in Washington? When we wonder this, we need to rediscover the hope that people have been in our shoes before and they've lived to cross those bridges.

Personally, I find that hope in thinking about a trip I took during my campaign for the U.S. Senate.

About a week after the primary, Dick Durbin and I embarked on a nineteen-city tour of Southern Illinois. And one of the towns we went to was a place called Cairo, which, as many of you might know, achieved a certain notoriety during the late '60s and early '70s as having one of the worst racial climates in the country. You had an active white citizen's council there, you had cross burnings, Jewish families were being harassed, you had segregated schools, race riots, you name it—it was going on in Cairo.

And we're riding down to Cairo and Dick Durbin turns to me and says,

> "Let me tell you about the first time I went to Cairo. It was about 30 years ago. I was 23 years old and Paul Simon, who was Lieutenant Governor at the time, sent me down there to investigate what could be done to improve the racial climate in Cairo."

And Dick tells me how he diligently goes down there and gets picked up by a local resident who takes him to his motel. And as Dick's getting out of the car, the driver says,

> "Excuse me, let me just give you a piece of advice. Don't use the phone in your motel room because the switchboard operator is a member of the white citizen's council, and they'll report on anything you do."

Well, this obviously makes Dick Durbin upset, but he's a brave young man, so he checks in to his room, unpacks his bags, and a few minutes later he hears a knock on the door. He opens up the door and there's a guy standing there who just stares at Dick for a second, and then says, "What the hell are you doing here?" and walks away.

Well, now Dick is really feeling concerned and so am I because as he's telling me this story, we're pulling in to Cairo. So I'm wondering what kind of reception we're going to get. And we wind our way through the town and we go past the old courthouse, take a turn and suddenly we're in a big parking lot and about 300 people are standing there. About a fourth of them are black and three-fourths are white and they all are about the age where they would have been active participants in the epic struggle that had taken place thirty years earlier.

And as we pull closer, I see something. All of these people are wearing these little buttons that say "Obama for U.S. Senate." And they start smiling. And they start waving. And Dick and I looked at each other and didn't have to say a thing. Because if you told Dick thirty years ago that he—the son of Lithuania immigrants born into very modest means in East St. Louis—would be returning to Cairo as a sitting United States Senator, and that he would have in tow a black guy born in Hawaii with a father from Kenya and a mother from Kansas named Barack Obama, no one would have believed it.

But it happened. And it happened because John Lewis and scores of brave Americans stood on that bridge and lived to cross it.

You know, two weeks after Bloody Sunday, when the march finally reached Montgomery, Martin Luther King Jr. spoke to the crowd of thousands and said "The arc of the moral universe is long, but it bends towards justice." He's right, but you know what? It doesn't bend on its own. It bends because we help it bend that way. Because people like John Lewis and Martin Luther King and Rosa Parks and thousands of ordinary Americans with extraordinary courage have helped bend it that way. And as their examples call out to us from across the generations, we continue to progress as a people because they inspire us to take our own two hands and bend that arc.

PRIVACY AND FREEDOM
A Speech To The American Library Association
June 27, 2005

(Chicago, Illinois) Barack Obama delivered this keynote speech at the American Library Association's Annual Conference, taking as his theme Privacy and Freedom: *I want to work with you to insure that libraries continue to be sanctuaries for learning, where we are free to read and consider what we please, without the fear of Big Brother peering menacingly over our shoulders.*

It is a pleasure to address you today because of what libraries represent. More than a building that houses books and data, the library has always been a window to a larger world—a place where we've always come to discover big ideas and profound concepts that help move the American story forward.

And at a time when truth and science are constantly being challenged by political agendas and ideologies, a time where so many refuse to teach evolution in our schools, where fake science is used to beat back attempts to curb global warming or fund life-saving research, libraries remind us that truth isn't about who yells the loudest, but who has the right information. Because even as we're the most religious of people, America's innovative genius has always been preserved because we also have a deep faith in facts.

And so the moment we persuade a child, any child, to cross that threshold into a library, we've changed their lives forever, and for the better. This is an enormous force for good.

So I'm here to gratefully acknowledge the importance of libraries and the work you do. I also want to work with you to insure that libraries continue to be sanctuaries for learning, where we are free to read and consider what we please, without the fear of Big Brother peering menacingly over our shoulders.

Now, some of you might have heard about this speech I gave at the Democratic Convention last summer. It ended up making some news here and there, and one of the lines that people seem to remember was when I said that, "We don't like federal agents poking around our libraries in the red states."

What many people don't remember is that for years, librarians are the ones who've been on the frontlines of this fight for privacy and freedom. There have always been dark times in our history where America has strayed from the ideals that make us a great nation. But the question has always been, can we overcome? And you have always been a group of Americans who have answered a resounding "yes" to that question.

When political groups try to censor great works of literature, you're the ones putting *Huck Finn* and *Catcher in the Rye* back on the shelves, making sure that our right to free thought and free information is protected. And ever since we've had to worry about our own government looking over our shoulders in the library, you've been there to stand up and speak out on privacy issues. You're full-time defenders of the most fundamental American liberties, and for that, you deserve America's deepest gratitude.

You also deserve our protection. That's why I've been working with Republicans and Democrats to make sure we have a Patriot Act that helps us track down terrorists without trampling on our civil liberties. This is an issue that Washington always tries to make "either-or." Either we protect our people from terror or we protect our most cherished principles. But this kind of choice asks too little of us and assumes too little about America. We can harness new technologies and a new toughness to find terrorists before they strike while still protecting the very freedoms we're fighting for in the first place.

I know that some of you here have been subject to FBI or other law enforcement orders asking for reading records. And so I hope we can pass a provision like the House of Representatives did that would require federal agents to get these kinds of search warrants from a real judge in a real court, just like everyone else does. In the Senate, the bipartisan bill that we're working on, known as the SAFE Act, will prevent the federal government from freely rifling through emails and library records without first obtaining such a warrant. Giving law enforcement the tools they need to investigate suspicious activity is one thing, but doing it without the approval of our judicial system seriously jeopardizes the rights of all Americans and the ideals America stands for.

Now, in addition to the line about federal agents poking around in our libraries, there was also another line in the convention speech that received a lot of attention, a line I'd like to talk more about today. At one point in the speech, I mentioned that the people I've met all across Illinois know that government can't solve all their problems. They know that, quote, "parents have to parent, that children can't achieve unless we raise their expectations and turn off the television sets and eradicate the slander that says a black youth with a book is acting white."

I included this line in the speech because I believe that we have a serious challenge to meet. I believe that if we want to give our children the best possible chance in life, if we want to open doors of opportunity while they're young and teach them the skills they'll need to succeed later on, then one of our greatest responsibilities as citizens, as educators, and as parents, is to ensure that every American child can read and read well.

This isn't just another education debate where the answer lies somewhere between more money and less bureaucracy. It's a responsibility that begins at home—one that we need to take on before our kids ever step foot in a classroom, one that we need to carry through well into their teenage years.

That's because literacy is the most basic currency of the knowledge economy we're living in today. Only a few generations ago, it was okay to enter the workforce as a high school dropout who could only read at a third-grade level. Whether it was on a farm or in a factory, you could still hope to find a job that would allow you to pay the bills and raise your family.

But that economy is long gone. As revolutions in technology and communication began breaking down barriers between countries and connecting people all over the world, new jobs and industries that require more skill and knowledge have come to dominate the economy. Whether it's software design or computer engineering or financial analysis, corporations can locate these jobs anywhere there's an internet connection. And so, as countries like China and India continue to modernize their economies and educate their children longer and better, the competition American workers face will grow more intense, the necessary skills more demanding.

These new jobs are about what you know and how fast you can learn what you don't know. They require innovative thinking, detailed comprehension, and superior communication.

But before our children can even walk into an interview for one of these jobs, before they can ever fill out an application or earn the required college degree, they have to be able to pick up a book, read it, and understand it. Nothing is more basic, no ability more fundamental.

Reading is the gateway skill that makes all other learning possible, from complex word problems and the meaning of our history to scientific discovery and technological proficiency. In a knowledge economy where this kind of learning is necessary for survival, how can we send our kids out into the world if they're only reading at a fourth grade level?

I don't know, but we do. Day after day, year after year.

Right now, one out of every five adults in the United States can't read a simple story to their child. During the last twenty years or so, over ten million Americans reached the twelfth grade without having learned to read at a basic level.

But these literacy problems start far before high school. In 2000, only thirty-two percent of all fourth graders tested as reading proficient. And the story gets worse when you take race and income into consideration. Children from low-income families score twenty-seven points below the average reading level, while students from wealthy families score fifteen points above the average. And while only one in twelve white seventeen-year-olds has the ability to pick up the newspaper and understand the science section, for Hispanics the number jumps to one in fifty; for African-Americans it's one in one hundred.

In this new economy, teaching our kids just enough so that they can get through Dick and Jane isn't going to cut it. Over the last ten years, the average literacy required for all American occupations is projected to rise by fourteen percent. It's not enough just to recognize the words on the page anymore. The kind of literacy necessary for 21st Century employment requires detailed understanding and complex comprehension. But too many kids simply aren't learning at that level.

And yet, every year we pass more of these kids through school or watch as more dropout. These kids who will pore through the Help Wanted section and cross off job and after job that requires skills they just don't have. And others who will have to take that Help Wanted section, walk it over to someone else, and find the courage to ask, "Will you read this for me?"

We have to change our whole mindset in this country. We're living in a 21st Century knowledge economy, but our schools, our homes, and our culture are still based around 20th Century expectations. It might seem like we're doing kids a favor by teaching them just enough to count change and read a food label, but in this economy, it's doing them a huge disservice. Instead, we need to start setting high standards and inspirational examples for our children to follow. While there's plenty that can be done to improve our schools and reform education in America, this isn't just an issue where we can turn to the government and ask for help. Reading has to begin at home.

We know that children who start kindergarten with an awareness of letters and basic language sounds become better readers and face fewer challenges in the years ahead. We also know that the more reading material kids are exposed to at home, the better they score on reading tests throughout their lives. So we need to make investments in family literacy programs and early childhood education so that kids aren't left behind before they even go to school. And we need to get books in our kids' hands early and often.

I know that this is often easier said than done. Parents today still have the toughest job in the world—and no one ever thanks you enough for doing it. You're working longer and harder than ever, juggling job and family responsibilities, and trying to be everywhere at once. When you're home, you might try to get your kids to read, but you're competing with the other byproducts of the technological revolution: video games and DVDs that they just have to have, TVs in every room of the household. Children eight to eighteen now spend three hours a day watching TV, while they only spend forty-three minutes reading.

Our kids aren't just seeing these temptations at home—they're everywhere. Whether it's their friends or the people they see on TV or a general culture that glorifies anti-intellectualism, it's too easy for kids today to put down a book and turn their attention elsewhere. And it's too easy for the rest of us to make excuses for it—pretending that putting a baby in front of a DVD is educational, letting a twelve-year-old skip reading as long as he's playing good video games, or substituting dinner in front of the TV for family conversation.

We know that's not what our kids need. We know that's not what's best for them. And so as parents, we need to find the time and the energy to step in and find ways to help our kids love reading. We can read to them, talk to them about what they're reading and make time for this by turning off the TV ourselves.

Libraries can help parents with this. Knowing the constraints we face from busy schedules and a TV culture, we need to think outside the box here, to dream big like we always have in America. Right now, children come home from their first doctor's appointment with an extra bottle of formula. But imagine if they came home with their first library card or their first copy of *Goodnight Moon*?

What if it was as easy to get a book as it is to rent a DVD or pick up McDonald's? What if instead of a toy in every Happy Meal, there was a book? What if there were portable libraries that rolled through parks and playgrounds like ice cream trucks? Or kiosks in stores where you could borrow books? What if during the summer, when kids often lose much of the reading progress they've made during the year, every child had a list of books they had to read and talk about and an invitation to a summer reading club at the local library?

Libraries have a special role to play in our knowledge economy. Your institution has been and should be the place where parents and kids come to read together and learn together. We should take our kids here more, and we should make sure politicians aren't closing libraries down because they had to spend a few extra bucks on tax cuts instead.

Each of you has a role here too. You can get more kids to walk through your doors by building on the ideas so many of you are already pursuing—book clubs and contests, homework help and advertising your services throughout the community. In the years ahead, this is our challenge, and this must be our responsibility.

As a librarian or as a parent, every one of you here today can probably remember the look on a child's face after finishing a first book. They turn that last page and stare up at you with those wide eyes, and in that look you find such a sense of accomplishment and pride, of great potential and so much possibility.

And in that moment, there's nothing we want more than to nurture that hope, to make all those possibilities and all those opportunities real for our children, to have the ability to answer the question, "What can I be when I grow up?" with "Anything you want—anything you can dream of."

It's a hope that's as old as the American story itself. From the moment the first immigrants arrived on these shores, generations of parents have worked hard and sacrificed whatever is necessary so that their children could have the same chances they had, or the chances they never had. Because while we could never ensure that our children would be rich or successful, while we could never be positive that they would do better than their parents, America is about making it possible to give them the chance. To give every child the opportunity to try.

Education is still the foundation of this opportunity. And the most basic building block that holds that foundation together is still reading. At the dawn of the 21st Century, in a world where knowledge truly is power and literacy is the skill that unlocks the gates of opportunity and success, we all have a responsibility as parents and librarians, educators and citizens, to instill in our children a love of reading so that we can give them the chance to fulfill their dreams.

HONORING AMERICA'S VETERANS
A Speech To The American Legion
July 16, 2005

(Springfield, Illinois) Barack Obama delivered this speech at the American Legion Conference, taking as his theme the moral commitment America has to its war veterans: *It is not only our patriotic duty to provide this care, it is our moral duty at the most fundamental level—and we must rise to that challenge.*

Thank you. It's an honor to be here today with all of you Legionnaires.

Over the last few months and throughout the campaign, I've been able to travel the state and meet veterans from all across Illinois. And no matter how many stories of heroism I hear, I constantly find myself in awe of your service and inspired by your sacrifice.

Oliver Wendell Holmes once said that, "To fight out a war, you must believe something and want something with all your might." In America, we must never forget how lucky we are to have so many men and women who believe—who are willing to put aside their own pursuit of happiness, to subordinate their own sense of survival, for something bigger, something greater.

When many of you joined the Armed Forces, you had your whole lives ahead of you—birthdays and weddings, holidays with family and friends, successes not yet achieved. And yet, you were willing to leave all of that behind—perhaps forever—because you believed that your service would make it possible for the rest of us to live happily, safely, and freely.

And so it's this sense of obligation—of responsibility to one's fellow American—that we must honor when our veterans return and need our care and support. Since I joined the Veterans Committee, I've heard a lot of debate over funding and budget numbers, about what we can afford and where we can save money. But I know those aren't the first things that come to your mind when you think about taking care of America's veterans.

And they're not the first things that come to my mind either.

I think about my grandfather, who signed up for duty in World War II the day after Pearl Harbor. He marched across Europe in Patton's army, and when he came home, it was the education and opportunity offered by the GI Bill that allowed his family to build their own American Dream.

I think about stories like the one I heard from a veteran named Bill Allen, who told me that on a trip to Chicago, he actually saw homeless veterans fighting over access to the dumpsters.

And I think about people like Seamus Ahern, who I met during the campaign at a VFW hall in East Moline. He told me about how he'd joined the Marines because he was so proud of this country, and he felt that as a young person in his early twenties he wanted to give something back. We became friends and we kept in touch over e-mail while he was in Iraq. One day he sent me one that said, "I'm sorry I haven't written more often—I've been a little busy over here." I had to tell him, "Don't worry—I know you've got your hands full."

But as I listened to Seamus explain why he'd enlisted, the absolute faith he had in our country and its leaders, his devotion to duty and service, I thought this young man was all that any of us might hope for in a child. And then I asked myself: When Seamus comes home, will we serve him as well as he served us?

That's the question we should be asking ourselves when we talk about veterans' benefits and the veterans' budget. And that's the standard we should meet.

And so I ask: are we serving our veterans as well as they've served us when we find out that veterans' health care has been shortchanged by at least one billion dollars? A shortfall that could have meant veterans turned away from doctor's visits, veterans unable to pay their medical bills, or veterans refused the prosthetics they need to live normal lives?

Thankfully, we restored the funding in Congress so that none of this would happen. But let me be clear—the Department of Veterans Affairs should never be funded as an afterthought. Republicans and Democrats warned the administration that there may be a shortfall months ago, and so we shouldn't have to be scraping for change now to care for those who risked their lives to defend ours. It should be America's first priority.

And yet, you've all seen how we keep falling short. How disabled veterans are waiting hundreds of days just to get their claim processed. How wounded veterans in Illinois receive fewer disability benefits than those in New Mexico or Maine. When I first arrived in the Senate, and saw the *Chicago Sun-Times* report that ranked Illinois 49th in how much disability pay our veterans received, we decided to hold town hall meetings here in Springfield and in Chicago to hear directly from you. Well, you spoke, we relayed your concerns to VA Secretary Nicholson, he came out to see the problem for himself, and now we've increased our VA staff by twenty-seven percent so there are more caseworkers for each veteran.

But the benefits are still too low and the waits are still too long, and so we've got a ways to go. It's not enough to simply wave a flag and welcome our veterans with words of praise—we need to get serious about solving these problems and honoring their service. We held a hearing in Chicago about these issues just the other week, and I heard from a veteran whose hands had been crushed in an accident. Twenty years later he's still caught in the VA bureaucracy, trying to obtain disability benefits. Twenty years later. Meanwhile, we just learned that the VA's latest solution on disability disparities is to stop ranking which states are the best and worst. I don't know about you, but I don't think that burying bad news is any way deal with it.

If this is the best we can do for veterans who've already come home, what will we do for the hundreds of thousands who will, God-willing, return from Iraq and Afghanistan? Veterans already have difficulty accessing VA care, and none of us want those who are still fighting to be greeted by a system that tells them, "Thanks for fighting for your country—now take a number."

We know that soldiers are already coming home with Post Traumatic Stress Disorder, and we know that a recent Army study showed that one in six soldiers in Iraq reported symptoms of major depression. Some experts predict that more than 100,000 soldiers may need some kind of mental health treatment when they come home. For tens of thousands of others, the wounds they suffered in battle will need care that could last a lifetime. These brave men and women may not have survived earlier wars, but thanks to advances in technology, these young people not only have the chance to survive, but to live normal lives. But it's up to us to provide the resources to make that a reality.

It is not only our patriotic duty to provide this care, it is our moral duty at the most fundamental level—and we must rise to that challenge.

We've made some progress already. In Congress, with the help of the American Legion, I worked to ensure that our hospitalized soldiers don't get billed for their meals. And I've also sponsored the Sheltering All Veterans Everywhere Act, which would strengthen the VA programs our homeless vets need to get back on their feet. The American Legion has endorsed this bill, and so I hope we can work together on this and other initiatives in the future.

Over half a century ago, it was American Legion National Commander Harry Colmery who first sat down and wrote the legislation that would become the GI Bill of Rights—a bill that has since provided education and training for nearly eight million Americans, housing for nearly two million families, and led to the creation of the great American middle class. That was a bill that told our heroes, "When you come home, we're here for you, because we're all in this together."

Today, we shouldn't be scraping to find the bare minimum in benefits and health care for our veterans. And with the largest deployment of troops since Vietnam fighting for freedom in an increasingly dangerous world, we should be talking about a GI Bill for the 21st Century.

When veterans look to Congress for help, this is the kind of legislation they should hear about, not budget cuts and funding shortfalls.

It's time to reassess our priorities. We never hesitate to praise the service of our veterans and acknowledge the debt we owe them for their service, but now we must renew our commitment to them by increasing funding for the VA, and ensure that our veterans receive more than just words of praise, but also the health care and benefits they've earned.

George Washington once said, "The willingness with which our young people are likely to serve in any war, no matter how justified, shall be directly proportional to how they perceive veterans of earlier wars were treated and appreciated by our nation."

Washington understood then what every veteran here knows now—that when we make the decision to send our troops to war, we also make the decision to care for them, to speak for them, and to think of them—always—when they come.

Thank you and God Bless you.

IF WE STAND TOGETHER,
WE RISE TOGETHER
A Speech To The AFL- CIO National Convention
July 25, 2005

(Chicago, Illinois) Barack Obama delivered this speech at the AFL-CIO's Fiftieth Anniversary National Convention, taking as his theme the plight of the American worker in the global economy: *At a time of such insecurity and vulnerability, there has never been a greater need for a strong labor movement to stand up for American workers.*

It would be naive of me to start without acknowledging what's been on everyone's mind during this convention. As America tries to find its way in a global economy, we meet here at a challenging time for the labor movement. There are questions of strategy and tactics, leadership and power. And I can imagine that many of you are anxious not only about labor's future, but yours. You're wondering, will I be able to leave my children a better world than I was given? Will I be able to save enough to send them to college or plan for a secure retirement? Will my job even be there tomorrow? Who will stand up for me in this new world?

In this time of change and uncertainty, these questions are expected—but they are by no means unique.

From the earliest days of our founding, they have been asked and then answered by Americans who have stood in your shoes and shared your concerns about the future.

At the heyday of the Industrial Revolution, millions from around the world flocked to this very city in search of opportunity. Immigrants from Europe, African-Americans from the Jim Crow South, and ethnic groups from every corner of America made their home in these neighborhoods and a living from the mills and factories that crowded a bustling Chicago.

The work was brutal and the pay was low, but none more so than on the South Side between Halsted and Ashland Avenue, where you could smell the stench of the meatpacking stockyards from miles away.

50,000 worked in what Upton Sinclair would later call "The Jungle," under some of the most dangerous and oppressive conditions in America. Twice the workers tried to organize, and twice they were ferociously beaten back by employers willing to use violence, race-baiting, and starvation in order to keep wages at 32 cents an hour.

But these workers made a choice—a choice that this would not be their future. And so in 1937, as the CIO begin organizing mass industries all across America, meatpacking workers began to follow their lead.

Imagine—these people would slave away in these plants all day long, freezing in the winter and sweltering in the summer, watching coworkers get their bones crushed in machines and friends get fired for even uttering the word "union"—and yet after they punched their card at the end of the day, they organized. They went to meetings and they passed out leaflets. They put aside decades of ethnic and racial tension and elected women, African-Americans, and immigrants to leadership positions so that they could speak with one voice.

They could have accepted their lot in life or waited for someone else to save them. Through their actions they risked life and living.

They chose to act.

In time, they won. It started with victories as small as putting fans on the factory floor, and ended with paid holidays, and wage increases, and a seniority system, and pensions.

It started with hope, and it ended with the fulfillment of a long-held ideal. A humble band of laborers against an industrial giant—an unlikely triumph against the greatest odds—a story as American as any.

For this has always been the way with us—at the edge of despair, in the shadow of hopelessness, ordinary people make the extraordinary decision that if we stand together, we rise together.

And we do.

At the end of the Civil War, when farmers and their families began moving into the cities to work in the big factories that were sprouting up all across America, we had to decide: Do we do nothing and allow the captains of industry and robber barons to run roughshod over the economy and workers by competing to see who can pay the lowest wage at the worst working conditions? Or do we try to make the system work by setting up basic rules for the market, and instituting the first public schools, and busting up monopolies, and fighting so that working people could organize into unions?

Through strikes and sit-ins, petitions and rallies, and leaders who kept opportunity alive, we chose to act, and we rose together.

Years later, when the irrational exuberance of the Roaring Twenties came crashing down with the stock market, we had to decide: do we follow the call of leaders who would do nothing, or the call of a leader who, perhaps because of his physical paralysis, refused to accept political paralysis?

From Roosevelt's decision that political freedom would mean nothing without economic freedom to labor's tireless fight for that same principle, we chose to act—regulating the market, putting people back to work, expanding bargaining rights to include health care and a secure retirement—and together we rose.

Today, we face a challenge and a choice once more.

Too many of you have seen this challenge up close—when you drive by the old factory around lunchtime and no one walks out anymore. When you can't get that raise or that health care plan you hoped for because your employer is competing with companies who pay foreign workers a fraction of what you make.

I saw it during the campaign when I met the union guys who used to work at the Maytag plant down in Galesburg and now wonder what they're gonna do at fifty-five years old without a pension or health care; when I met the man whose son needs a new liver but doesn't know if he can afford it when the kid gets to the top of the transplant list.

It's as if someone changed the rules in the middle of the game and no one bothered to tell them.

But as we all know, the rules have changed.

It started with technology and automation that rendered entire occupations obsolete. Then companies were able to pick up and move their factories to the developing world, where workers are a lot cheaper than they are in the U.S. Now, advances in technology and communication mean that businesses not only have the ability to move jobs wherever there's a factory, but wherever there's an internet connection.

These changes have transformed the American worker into a kind of global free agent—if you can learn the right skills and get a great education, you can out-compete any worker in the world for the high-paying jobs of tomorrow. But it also means that the days of lifetime employment at a company that provided wages, health care, and pensions you can bargain for are coming to an end.

At a time of such insecurity and vulnerability, there has never been a greater need for a strong labor movement to stand up for American workers.

But the question we need to answer is: how will this movement and our people win in this new global economy?

Once again, we face a choice. We know that globalization is not just another issue you can be for or against—it's here to stay. And so the question is not whether we can stop it, but how we respond to it.

Some answers are clear. When you have an administration that says "no" to a labor-friendly labor board, "no" to organizing rights, "no" to overtime pay, and "no" to a higher minimum wage, you say "no" to that administration and put someone else in office.

The Bush Administration's philosophy says we can't do much about the new challenges we face as a nation. And since there is not much to do about global competition, the best that can be done is to give everyone one big refund on their government—divvy it up into individual portions, hand it out, and encourage everyone to use their share to go buy their own health care, their own retirement plan, their own child care, education, and so forth.

In Washington, they call this the Ownership Society. But in our past there has been another term for it—Social Darwinism, every man and woman for him or herself. It's a tempting idea, because it doesn't require much thought or ingenuity. It allows us to say to those whose health care or tuition may rise faster than they can afford—tough luck. It allows us to say to the factory workers who have lost their job—life isn't fair. It let's us say to the child born into poverty—pull yourself up by your bootstraps.

But there is a problem. It won't work. It ignores our history. It ignores the fact that it has been government research and investment that made the railways and the internet possible. It has been the creation of a massive middle class, through decent wages and benefits and public schools, that has allowed all of us to prosper. It has been the ability of working men and women to join together in unions and demand justice and opportunity that has kept America upwardly mobile.

Our economic dominance has always depended on individual initiative and belief in the free market; it has also depended on our sense of mutual regard for each other, the idea that everybody has a stake in the country, that we're all in it together and everybody's got a shot at opportunity.

So part of the fight is political—and part of the solution is to strengthen the right to organize across all industries and professions.

But it's not enough just to say "no" to Bush. They may not have helped, and they may have made things worse, but they did not cause globalization. And no matter what comes out of this convention, the labor movement must squarely confront the fact that the economy is changing. The old ways of doing business are not working, and we must have a strategy that meets these new challenges.

I won't stand up here and say that coming up with this strategy will be easy, or pretend to know all the answers.

But part of the answer is recognizing that while unions and government can no longer provide this opportunity in the form of lifetime employment, they can ensure that every American worker has lifetime employability in this new economy.

That means fixing our schools to make sure every child in America has the education and the skills they need to compete—and that college is affordable for every American who wants to go. And it means that unions can play a real role in finally creating a real system of lifelong learning so that workers who lose a job really can retrain for other high-wage jobs.

It means spurring job creation and innovation by investing our resources into research and development projects, not cutting them. It means investing in broadband and in medical technology; working with local communities to create centers of innovation. It's time to fuel the genius and the innovation that will lead to the new jobs and new industries of the future.

Right now, all across America, there are amazing discoveries being made. At Pittsburgh's Carnegie Mellon University, researchers have developed a virtual algebra tutor that has helped inner-city kids in under-served schools raise their scores an entire letter grade. In rural Virginia, telemedicine recently allowed a cardiologist 75 miles from the hospital to view an ultrasound and diagnose a congenital heart defect that required immediate medication, saving a young child's life. And in the very cornfields of Illinois, farmers are literally growing the biofuels that could ultimately run our cars on 500 miles per gallon. Breakthroughs like these won't just improve our lives, they'll create thousands of jobs that could be filled by American workers trained with new skills and a world-class education.

In this new economy, we should be able to tell workers that no matter where you work or how many times you switch jobs, you will have health care and a pension you can take with you always. We'll never rise together if we allow medical bills to swallow family budgets or let people retire penniless after a lifetime of hard work, and so today we must demand that when it comes to commitments made to working men and women on health care and pensions, a promise made is a promise kept.

Our vision of America is not one where a big government runs our lives; it's one that gives every American the opportunity to make the most of their lives. It's not one that tells us we're on our own; it's one that realizes that we rise or fall together as one people.

And yet, we also know that, in the end, neither policy nor politics can replace heart and courage in the struggle you now face. Because in the brief history of the American experiment, it has been the ability of ordinary Americans to act on both that has allowed our nation to achieve extraordinary things.

It's why farmers put down their ploughs and picked up arms to overthrow an Empire for the sake of an idea. It's why young men and women would take Freedom Rides down South to work for the Civil Rights movement. And it's why workers would stand cold, hungry, and penniless on picket lines until their labor was treated with the dignity it deserved.

Almost a century earlier, during the struggle for the soul of Chicago's stockyards, Hank Johnson, a leading African-American union organizer, told a crowd of laborers that in the end, speeches don't make unions. He said that "the real job of organizing has to be done everyday by the men and women who work right in the plant."

That's as true today as it was then. The real job of organizing working America—politics and policy, vision and mission, heart and soul—belongs to each of you. And if you have the courage to succeed, labor will rise again. America will rise again. And hope will rise again. Thank you and God Bless you.

WORLD-CLASS EDUCATION
Teaching Our Kids In The Twenty-First Century
October 25, 2005

(Washington, D.C.) Barack Obama delivered this speech at the "Teaching Our Kids In The Twenty-First Century" event sponsored by the progressive Center For American Progress: *It's time for this nation to rededicate itself to the ideal of a world-class education for every American child.*

The other day, I was reading through Jonathan Kozol's new book, *Shame of a Nation*. In it, he talks about his recent travels to schools across America, and how fifty years after *Brown v. Board of Education*, we have an education system in this country that is still visibly separate and painfully unequal.

At one point, Kozol tells about his trip to Fremont High School in Los Angeles, where he meets some children who explain with heart-wrenching honesty what living in this system is like. One girl told him that she'd taken hairdressing twice, because there were actually two different levels offered by the high school. The first was in hairstyling, the other in braiding.

Another girl, Mireya, listened as her friend told this story. And she began to cry. When asked what was wrong, she said,

> "I don't want to take hairdressing. I did not need sewing either. I knew how to sew. My mother is a seamstress in a factory. I'm trying to go to college. I don't need to sew to go to college. My mother sews. I hoped for something else."

I hoped for something else.

It's a simple dream, but it speaks to us so powerfully because it is our dream—one that exists at the very center of the American experience. One that says if you're willing to work hard and take responsibility, then you'll have the chance to reach for something else, for something better.

The ideal of public education has always been at the heart of this bargain. From the moment the earliest Americans stepped out from the shadows of tyranny and built the first free schools in the towns of New England and across the Southern plains, it was the driving force behind Thomas Jefferson's declaration that "talent and virtue, needed in a free society, should be educated regardless of wealth, birth or other accidental condition."

It's a bargain our government kept as we moved from a nation of farms to a nation of factories, setting up a system of free public high schools to give every American the chance to participate in the new economy. It's a bargain we expanded after World War II, when we sent over two million returning heroes to college on the GI Bill, creating the largest middle class in history.

And even when our government refused to hold up its end of this bargain, when America fell short of its promise and forced Linda Brown to walk miles to a dilapidated Topeka school because she wasn't allowed in the well-off, white-only school near her house—even then, ordinary people marched and bled, they took to the streets and fought in the courts, they stood up and spoke out until the day when the arrival of nine little children at a school in Little Rock made real the decision that, in America, separate could never be equal. Because, in America, it's the promise of a good education for all that makes it possible for any child to transcend the barriers of race or class or background and achieve their God-given potential.

In this country, it is education that allows our children to hope for something else.

And as the 21st Century unfolds, we are called once again to make real this hope—to meet the new challenges of a global economy by carrying forth the ideals of progress and opportunity through public education in America.

We now live in a world where the most valuable skill you can sell is knowledge. Revolutions in technology and communication have created an entire economy of high-tech, high-wage jobs that can be located anywhere there's an internet connection. And today, a child in Chicago is not only competing for jobs with one in Boston, but thousands more in Bangalore and Beijing who are being educated longer and better than ever before.

America is in danger of losing this competition. We now have one of the highest high school dropout rates of any industrialized country. By twelfth grade, our children score lower on their math and science tests than most other kids in the world. And today, countries like China are graduating eight times as many engineers as we do.

And yet, as these fundamental changes are occurring all around us, we still hear about schools that are giving students the choice between hairstyling and braiding.

Let's be clear—we are failing too many of our children. We're sending them out into a 21st Century economy by sending them through the doors of 20th Century schools.

Right now, six million middle and high school students are reading at levels significantly below their grade level. Half of all teenagers can't understand basic fractions; half of all nine-year-olds can't perform basic multiplication or division. For some students, the data is even worse: almost sixty percent of African-American fourth graders can't read at even the basic level. And by eighth grade, nearly nine in ten African-American and Latino students are not proficient in math. More students than ever are taking college entrance exams, but these tests are showing that only twenty percent are prepared to take college-level classes in English, math, and science. For African-American students, the figure dips to just ten percent.

What happens to these kids? What happens to the one in four eighth graders who never go on to finish high school in five years? What happens to the one in two high school graduates who never go on to college?

Thirty or forty years ago, they may have gone on to find a factory job that could pay the bills and support a family. But we no longer live in that world. Today, the average salary of a high school graduate is only $33,000 a year. For high school dropouts, it's even closer to the poverty line—just $25,000.

If we do nothing about this, if we accept this kind of economy; this kind of society, we face a future where the ideal of American meritocracy could turn into an American myth. A future that's not only morally unacceptable for our children, but economically untenable for a nation that finds itself in a globalized world, as countries who are out-educating us today out-compete our workers tomorrow.

Now, the American people understand that government alone can't meet this challenge. They understand that we need to transform our educational culture from one of complacency to one that constantly strives for excellence. And they understand that government cannot replace parents as the primary motivator for the hard work and commitment that excellence requires.

But they also know that government, through the public schools, plays a critical role. And what they've seen from government for close to two decades is not innovation or bold calls to action. Instead, what they've seen is inaction and tinkering around the edges of our education system—a paralysis that is fueled by ideological battles that are as outdated as they are predictable.

You know the arguments. On one side, you'll hear conservatives who will look at children without textbooks and classrooms without computers and say money doesn't matter. On the other side, you'll find liberals who will look at failing test scores and failing schools and not realize how much reform matters. One side will blame teachers, and the other side will never ask them to change. Some will say that no matter what you do, some children just can't learn. Others will make excuses for them when they won't learn.

Some will say that the same public school system that succeeded for generations must now be dismantled and privatized, no matter who it leaves behind. And others will defend the status quo in these schools even when they fail to teach our kids.

Like most ideological debates, this one assumes that there's an "either-or" answer to our education problems. Either we need to pour more money into the system, or we need to reform it with more tests and standards.

But we don't make much progress for our kids when we constrain ourselves like this. It appeared for a brief moment that the President, working with leaders like Senator Kennedy, understood this, and many of us were initially encouraged by the passage of "No Child Left Behind." It may not be popular to say in Democratic circles, but there were good elements to this bill: its emphasis on the achievement gap, raising standards, and accountability. Unfortunately, because of failures in implementation, particularly its failure to provide adequate funding and a failure to design better assessment tests that provide a clearer path for schools to raise achievement, the bill's promise is not yet fulfilled.

The shortcomings of NCLB shouldn't end the conversation, however. They should be the start of a conversation about how we can do better. Yes, it's a moral outrage that this Administration hasn't come through with the funding for what it claims has been its number one domestic priority. But to wage war against the entire law for that reason is not an education policy, and Democrats need to realize that.

If we truly believe in our public schools, then we have a moral responsibility to do better—to break the "either-or" mentality around school reform, and embrace a "both-and" mentality. Good schools will require both the structural reform and the resources necessary to prepare our kids for the future.

It's not as if innovation isn't taking place around the country. It's taking place in wealthier schools, like Illinois' Adlai Stevenson High School, which has one of the highest percentages of students taking AP exams in the country, and California's New Tech High, which puts a computer in front of every child. But it's also taking place in schools where large majorities of children find themselves below the poverty line yet above the national average in achievement—places like Newark's Branch Brook Elementary and Chicago's Carson Elementary School.

The problem is that we are not applying what we've learned from these successes to inform national policy. We need new vision for education in America—one where we move past ideology to experiment with the latest reforms, measure the results, and make policy decisions based on what works and what doesn't.

Now, if we are going to learn from schools that work, we must begin by admitting the obvious—money matters. In too many places, kids are going to school in trailers where rats are more numerous than computers. Smaller classes, books and lab supplies, better paid teachers, modernized buildings with the latest technology—all of this is critical if we are serious about educating our next generation.

But money alone won't make a difference without reform. And by the way, we won't be able to muster the political will to get more money into the system unless taxpayers are convinced that the money will produce measurable results. Fortunately, those who work in the field know what reforms really work: a more challenging and rigorous curriculum with emphasis on math, science, and literacy skills. Longer hours and more days to give kids the time and attention they need to learn. Early childhood education for every child so they're not left behind before they even start school. Meaningful, performance-based assessments that can give us a fuller picture of how a student is doing. And putting effective teachers and transformative principals in front of our kids.

All of these reforms need to be scaled-up and replicated across the country. But in the time I have remaining, let me just talk about a few to point to what's possible, starting with one place where I think we can start making a big difference in education right now.

From the moment our children step into a classroom, new evidence shows that the single most important factor in determining their achievement today is not the color of their skin or where they come from; it's not who their parents are or how much money they have.

It's who their teacher is. It's the person who will brave some of the most difficult schools, the most challenging children, and accept the most meager compensation simply to give someone else the chance to succeed.

One study shows that two groups of students who started third grade at about the same level of math achievement finished fifth grade at vastly different levels. The group with the effective teacher saw their scores rise by nearly twenty-five percent. The group with the ineffective teacher actually saw their scores drop by twenty-five percent.

But even though we know how much teaching matters, in too many places we've abandoned our teachers, sending them into some of the most impoverished, underperforming schools with little experience or pay, little preparation or support. After a few years of experience, most will leave to pick wealthier, less challenging schools.

The result is that some of our neediest children end up with less-experienced, poorly-paid teachers who are far more likely to be teaching subjects in which they have no training. Minority students are twice as likely to have these teachers. In Illinois, students in high-poverty schools are more than three times as likely to have them. The "No Child Left Behind" law, which states that all kids should have highly qualified teachers, is supposed to correct this, but so far it hasn't, because no one's followed through on the promise.

If we hope to give our children a chance, it's time we start giving our teachers a chance. We can't change the whole country overnight. But what we can do is give more school districts the chance to revolutionize the way they approach teaching. By helping spark complete reform across an entire school district, we can learn what actually works for our kids and then replicate those policies throughout the country.

So here's what I'm proposing: the creation of what I call Innovation Districts. School districts from around the country that want to become seedbeds of reform would apply and we'd select the twenty with the best plans to put effective, supported teachers in all classrooms and increase achievement for all students. We'd offer these districts substantial new resources to do this, but in return, we'd ask them to try systemic new reforms. Above all, we'd require results.

In Innovation Districts, we'd ask for reforms in four broad areas: teaching, most importantly, but also how teachers use their time, what they teach, and what we can do to hold our schools accountable for achievement.

We'd begin by working with these districts to strengthen their teaching, and we'd start with recruitment. Right now we don't have nearly enough effective teachers in the places we need them most: urban and rural schools, and subject areas like math and science. One of the main reasons for this, cited by most teachers who leave the profession, is that no one gives them the necessary training and preparation.

Around the country, organizations like the Academy for Urban School Leadership in Chicago are changing this by recruiting and training new, highly-qualified teachers for some of the hardest-to-teach classrooms in the country. We need to expand this by giving districts help in creating new teacher academies that will partner with organizations like this to recruit effective teachers for low-performing, high-poverty schools. Each teacher would undergo an extensive training program before they begin, including classroom observation and participation.

After we recruit great teachers, we need to pay them better. Right now, teaching is one of the only professions where no matter how well you perform at your job, you're almost never rewarded for success. But with six-figure salaries luring away some of our most talented college graduates from some of our neediest schools, this needs to change. That's why teachers in these Innovation Districts who are successful in improving student achievement would receive substantial pay increases, as would those who choose to teach in the most troubled schools and the highest-need subject areas, like math and science. The city of Denver is trying pay increases in partnership with the local union, and when Chattanooga, Tennessee offered similar incentives for teachers who taught in high-need schools, student reading scores went up by over ten percent.

Of course, teachers don't just need more pay, they need more support. One thing I kept hearing when I visited Dodge Elementary School in Chicago is how much an encouraging principal or the advice of an experienced teacher can make a difference. That's why teachers would be paired with mentor teachers who've been there before. After a few years of experience, they'd then have the chance to become mentor teachers themselves.

And to help them deal with those few disruptive students who tend to slow down the rest of the class—a problem I hear about from teachers all the time—we'd expand innovative programs being used in states like Illinois that teach students about positive behavior.

Finally, we would also require Innovation Districts to work with their unions to uncover bureaucratic obstacles that leave poor kids without good teachers, including hiring, funding, and transfer policies. Districts would work with unions to tackle these problems so that we can provide every child with an effective teacher.

Beyond policies that help teachers specifically, we'd also ask Innovation Districts to try reforms that create a more effective teaching environment. To give teachers more time with their students and more time to learn from each other, these districts would be asked to restructure their schedules and implement either longer days or summer school. In addition to more learning, this would provide kids a safe educational environment while their parents are at work.

And we'd make sure that in every school district across the country, educators are teaching a curriculum that will prepare our kids for the global economy. In many states, students are taught the anatomy of a flower as many as six times over the course of their education. Yet, they are never taught what they need to become a productive citizen in a global economy—like computer technology, how the economy works, why skyscrapers stand, or how to design a new product. Some states are successfully using this kind of project-based learning to give our kids real world, hands-on experience in the fields of science, technology, engineering, and math. We will provide funding for more of this learning in more of our schools.

To hold schools and teachers accountable for the results of all these reforms, Innovation Districts would be asked to support schools that succeed and shut down those that don't. To find out what works and what doesn't, we'd provide them with powerful data and technology, and also give them the option of partnering with local universities to help them improve performance, like what happens at the University of Chicago's Urban Education Initiative. Schools that raise student achievement would be given bonuses. For schools that don't improve, the districts would close them and replace them with new, smaller schools that can replicate some of the successful reforms taking place elsewhere. Entire districts that do not improve would be removed from the program.

These reforms would take an important first step toward fixing our broken system by putting qualified, supported teachers in the schools that need them most. But beyond that, they would show us the progress we can make when money is well spent. And they would allow us to finally break free from the "either-or" mentality that's put bureaucracy and ideology ahead of what works, ahead of what's best for our kids.

When it comes to education, the time for excuses has passed—for all of us.

During my visit to Dodge Elementary, I was able to speak with a few of the teachers about some of the challenges they're facing in educating their students. And one teacher mentioned to me that in one of the biggest obstacles in her view is what she referred to as the "These Kids" syndrome.

She said that when it comes to educating students today, people always seem to find a million excuses for why "these kids" can't learn. That you'll hear how "these kids are nothing but trouble," or "these kids come from tough backgrounds," or "these kids don't want to learn." And the more people talk about them as "these kids," the easier it is for "these kids" to become somebody else's problem.

But of course, the children in this country—the children in Dodge Elementary, and South Central L.A., and rural Arkansas, and suburban Maryland—they are not "these kids." They are our kids. They want a chance to achieve—and each of us has a responsibility to give them that chance.

In the end, children succeed because, somewhere along the way, a parent or teacher instills in them the belief that they can. That they're able to. That they're worth it.

At Earhart Elementary in Chicago, one little girl, raised by a single mom from a poor background, was asked the secret to her academic success. She said,

> "I just study hard every night because I like learning. My teacher wants me to be a good student, and so does my mother. I don't want to let them down."

In the months and years to come, it's time for this nation to rededicate itself to the ideal of a world class education for every American child. It's time to let our kids hope for something else. It's time to instill the belief in every child that they can succeed, and then make sure we make good on the promise to never let them down.

THE LEGACY OF ROBERT F. KENNEDY
The Robert F. Kennedy Human Rights Award
November 16, 2005

(Washington, D.C.) Barack Obama delivered this keynote speech at the *Robert F. Kennedy Human Rights Award* ceremony, taking as his theme the idealism of the late Robert Kennedy: *It was an idealism not based in rigid ideology. Yes, he believed that government is a force for good—but not the only force. He distrusted big bureaucracies, and knew that change erupts from the will of free people in a free society, that it comes not only from new programs, but new attitudes as well.*

Thank you. It's an honor to be here today....

I come to this with tremendous humility. I was only seven when Bobby Kennedy died. Many of the people in this room knew him as brother, as husband, as father, as friend.

I knew him only as an icon. In that sense, it is a distance I share with most of the people who now work in this Capitol, – many of whom were not even born when Bobby Kennedy died. But what's interesting is that if you go throughout the offices in the Capitol, everywhere you'll find photographs of Kennedy, or collections of his speeches, or some other memento of his life.

Why is this? Why is it that this man who was never President, who was our Attorney General for only three years, who was New York's junior Senator for just three and a half, still calls to us today? Still inspires our debate with his words, animates our politics with his ideas, and calls us to make gentle the life of a world that's too often coarse and unforgiving?

Obviously, much has to do with charisma and eloquence—that unique ability, rare for most but common among Kennedys, to sum up the hopes and dreams of the most diverse nation on Earth with a simple phrase or sentence, to inspire even the most apathetic observers of American life.

Part of it is his youth—both the time of life and the state of mind that dared us to hope that even after John was killed, even after we lost King, there would come a younger, energetic Kennedy who could make us believe again.

But beyond these qualities, there's something more.

Within the confines of these walls and the boundaries of this city, it becomes very easy to play small-ball politics. Somewhere between the partisan deadlock and the twenty-four hour news cycles, the contrived talking points, and the focus on the sensational over the substantive—issues of war and poverty, hopelessness, and lawlessness become problems to be managed, not crises to be solved. They become fodder for the Sunday show scrum, not places to find genuine consensus and compromise. And so, at some point, we stop reaching for the possible and resign ourselves to that which is most probable.

This is what happens in Washington.

And yet, as this goes on, somewhere another child goes hungry in a neighborhood just blocks away from one where a family is too full to eat another bite. Somewhere another hurricane survivor still searches for a home to return to or a school for her daughter. Somewhere another twelve-year-old is gunned down by an assailant who used to be his kindergarten playmate, and another parent loses their child on the streets of Tikrit.

But somewhere, there have also always been people who believe that this isn't the way it was supposed to be—that things should be different in America. People who believe that while evil and suffering will always exist, this is a country that has been fueled by small miracles and boundless dreams—a place where we're not afraid to face down the greatest challenges in pursuit of the greater good, a place where, against all odds, we overcome.

Bobby Kennedy was one of these people.

In a nation torn by war and divided against itself, he was able to look us in the eye and tell us that no matter how many cities burned with violence, no matter how persistent the poverty or the racism, no matter how far adrift America strayed, hope would come again.

It was an idealism not based in rigid ideology. Yes, he believed that government is a force for good, but not the only force. He distrusted big bureaucracies, and knew that change erupts from the will of free people in a free society, that it comes not only from new programs, but new attitudes as well.

And Kennedy's was not a pie-in-the-sky-type idealism either. He believed we would always face real enemies, and that there was no quick or perfect fix to the turmoil of the 1960s.

Rather, the idealism of Robert Kennedy—the unfinished legacy that calls us still—is a fundamental belief in the continued perfection of American ideals.

It's a belief that says if this nation was truly founded on the principles of freedom and equality, it could not sit idly by while millions were shackled because of the color of their skin. That if we are to shine as a beacon of hope to the rest of the world, we must be respected not just for the might of our military, but for the reach of our ideals. That if this is a land where destiny is not determined by birth or circumstance, we have a duty to ensure that the child of a millionaire and the child of a welfare mom have the same chance in life. That if, out of many, we are truly one, then we must not limit ourselves to the pursuit of selfish gain, but that which will help all Americans rise together.

We have not always lived up to these ideals and we may fail again in the future, but this legacy calls on us to try. And the reason it does—the reason we still hear the echo of not only Bobby's words, but John's and King's and Roosevelt's and Lincoln's before him—is because they stand in such stark contrast to the place in which we find ourselves today.

It's the timidity of politics that's holding us back right now, the politics of "can't-do" and "oh-well." An energy crisis that jeopardizes our security and our economy? No magic wand to fix it, we're told. Thousands of jobs vanishing overseas? It's actually healthier for the economy that way. Three days late to the worst natural disaster in American history? Brownie, you're doing a heck of a job.

And of course, if nothing can be done to solve the problems we face, if we have no collective responsibility to look out for one another, then the next logical step is to give everyone one big refund on their government—divvy it up into individual tax breaks, hand 'em out, and encourage everyone to go buy their own health care, their own retirement plan, their own child care, their own schools, their own roads, their own levees.

We know this as the Ownership Society. But in our past there has been another term for it—Social Darwinism—every man or women for him or herself. It allows us to say to those whose health care or tuition may rise faster than they can afford—tough luck. It allows us to say to the child who was born into poverty—pull yourself up by your bootstraps. It let's us say to the workers who lose their job when the factory shuts down—you're on your own.

But there is a problem. It won't work. It ignores our history. Yes, our greatness as a nation has depended on individual initiative, on a belief in the free market. But it has also depended on our sense of mutual regard for each other, the idea that everybody has a stake in the country, that we're all in it together and everybody's got a shot at opportunity.

Robert Kennedy reminded us of this. He reminds us still. He reminds us that we don't need to wait for a hurricane to know that Third World living conditions in the middle of an American city make us all poorer. We don't need to wait for the 3000th death of someone else's child in Iraq to make us realize that a war without an exit strategy puts all of our families in jeopardy. We don't have to accept the diminishment of the American Dream in this country now, or ever.

It's time for us to meet the whys of today with the why nots we often quote but rarely live—to answer "why hunger" and "why homeless," "why violence" and "why despair" with "why not good jobs and living wages," "why not better health care and world class schools," "why not a country where we make possible the potential that exists in every human being?"

If he were here today, I think it would be hard to place Robert F. Kennedy into any of the categories that so often constrain us politically. He was a fervent anti-communist but knew diplomacy was our way out of the Cuban Missile Crisis. He sought to wage the war on poverty but with local partnerships and community activism. He was at once both hard-headed and big-hearted.

And yet, his was not a centrism in the sense of finding a middle road or a certain point on the ideological spectrum. His was a politics that, at its heart, was deeply moral, based on the notion that in this world, there is right and there is wrong, and it's our job to organize our laws and our lives around recognizing the difference.

When RFK made his famous trip to the Mississippi Delta with Charles Evers in 1967, the story is often told about the destitute they encountered as they walked from shack to shack. As they walk into one with hardly a ceiling and a floor full of holes, Kennedy sees a small child with a swollen stomach sitting in the corner. He tries and tries to talk to this child again and again, but he gets no response, no movement, not even a look of awareness. Just a blank stare from cold, wide eyes so battered by poverty that they're barely alive.

And at that point we're told that Kennedy begins to cry. And he turns to Evers and asks, "How can a country like this allow it?" and Evers responds, "Maybe they just don't know."

Bobby Kennedy spent his life making sure that we knew—not only to wake us from indifference and face us with the darkness we let slip into our own backyard, but to bring us the good news that we have it within our power to change all this, to write our own destiny. Because we are a people of hope. Because we are Americans.

This is the good news we still hear all these years later, the message that still points us down the road that Bobby Kennedy never finished traveling. It's a road I hope our politics and our country begin to take in the months and years to come.

THE COMING STORM
Speech to The Newspaper Association of America
April 3, 2006

(Chicago, Illinois) Barack Obama delivered this speech at the Newspaper Association of America, taking as his theme global warming and the need for energy independence: *Climate change may be unleashing the forces of nature, but we can't forget that this has been accelerated by man and can be slowed by man too.*

In April of 2005, Elizabeth Kolbert did a series of articles for *The New Yorker* about climate change. In one of those articles, she tells a very interesting story about some of the effects we're already seeing from global warming.

About fifteen years ago, in the furthest reaches of Alaska, the people of a small, thousand-year-old, oceanfront hunting village noticed something odd. The ice that surrounded and protected the village, which is only twenty feet above sea level, began to grow slushy and weak. Soon, it began to freeze much later in the fall and melt much earlier in the spring.

As the ice continued to melt away at an alarming pace during the 1990s, the village began to lose the protection it offered and became more vulnerable to storm surges. In 1997, the town completely lost a hundred-twenty-five-foot-wide strip of land at its northern edge. In 2001, a storm with twelve-foot waves destroyed dozens of homes. And finally, in the summer of 2002, with the storms intensifying, the ice melting, and the land shrinking all around them, the residents of Shishmaref were forced to move their entire town miles inland, abandoning their homes forever.

The story of "The Village That Disappeared" is by no means isolated.

And it is by no means over.

All across the world, in every kind of environment and region known to man, increasingly dangerous weather patterns and devastating storms are abruptly putting an end to the long-running debate over whether or not climate change is real. Not only is it real, it's here, and its effects are giving rise to a frighteningly new global phenomenon: the man-made natural disaster.

For decades, we've been warned by legions of scientists and mountains of evidence that this was coming, that we couldn't just keep burning fossil fuels and contribute to the changing atmosphere without consequence. And yet, for decades, far too many have ignored the warnings, either dismissing the science as a hoax or believing that it was the concern of enviros looking to save polar bears and rainforests.

But today, we're seeing that climate change is about more than a few unseasonably mild winters or hot summers. It's about the chain of natural catastrophes and devastating weather patterns that global warming is beginning to set off around the world, the frequency and intensity of which are breaking records thousands of years old.

In Washington, issues come and go with the political winds. And they are generally covered through that prism: Who's up and who's down? Which party benefits? Which party loses?

But in these superficial exchanges, we often lose sight of the real and lasting meaning of the decisions we make and those we defer. The issue of climate change is one that we ignore at our own peril.

There may still be disputes about exactly how much we're contributing to the warming of the earth's atmosphere and how much is naturally occurring, but what we can be scientifically certain of is that our continued use of fossil fuels is pushing us to a point of no return. And unless we free ourselves from a dependence on these fossil fuels and chart a new course on energy in this country, we are condemning future generations to global catastrophe.

Just think about some of the trends we've seen.

Since 1980, we've experienced nineteen of the twenty hottest years on record, with 2005 being the hottest ever.

These high temperatures are drying up already dry land, causing unprecedented drought that's ruining crops, devastating farmers and spreading famine to already poor parts of the world. Over the last four decades, the percentage of the Earth's surface suffering drought has more than doubled. In the United States, the drought we experienced in 2002 was the worst in forty years. And in Africa, more rivers are beginning to dry up, threatening the water supply across the continent.

As more land becomes parched, more forests are starting to burn. Across Indonesia, throughout Alaska, and in the Western United States, wildfires have raged in recent years like never before. A new record was set in 2002, as more than 7 million acres burned from Oregon down to Arizona.

And while the situation on the land may look ugly, what's going on in the oceans is even worse. Hurricanes and typhoons thrive in warm water, and as the temperature has risen, so has the intensity of these storms. In the last thirty-five years, the percentage of Category 4 and 5 hurricanes has doubled, and the wind speed and duration of these storms has jumped fifty percent. A hurricane showed up in the South Atlantic recently when scientists said it could never happen. Last year, Japan set a new record when it suffered its tenth typhoon and the United States set a record for the most tornadoes we've ever had. And, at one point, Hurricane Wilma was the most powerful storm ever measured.

These are all frightening situations, but perhaps none more so than what is beginning to occur at the North and South Poles. There, a satellite image from space or a trip to the region shows indisputable evidence that the polar ice caps are melting. But it's not just a slow, steady thaw that's been occurring over centuries, it's a rapidly accelerating meltdown that may eventually dump enough water into the ocean to annihilate coastal regions across the globe.

In 1996, a melting Greenland dumped about twenty-two cubic miles of water into the sea. Today, just ten years later, it's melting twice as fast. In real terms, this means that every single month, Greenland is dumping into the ocean an amount of water fifty-four times greater than the city of Los Angeles uses in an entire year. All in all, Greenland has enough ice to raise the global sea level twenty-three feet, making a New Orleans out of nearly every coastal city imaginable.

Indeed, the Alaskan village of Shishmaref could be just the beginning.

And yet, despite all the ominous harbingers of things to come, we do not have to stand by helplessly and accept this future. In fact, we can't afford to. Climate change may be unleashing the forces of nature, but we can't forget that this has been accelerated by man and can be slowed by man too.

By now, the culprit of this climate change is a familiar one, as is the solution. Last September, when I gave my first speech on energy, I talked about how our dependence on oil is hurting our economy, decimating our auto industry, and costing us millions of jobs. A few months ago, I discussed how the oil we import is jeopardizing our national security by keeping us tied to the world's most dangerous and unstable regimes. And when it comes to climate change, it's the fossil fuels we insist on burning—particularly oil—that are the single greatest cause of global warming and the damaging weather patterns that have been its result.

You'd think by now we'd get the point on energy dependence. Never has the failure to take on a single challenge so detrimentally affected nearly every aspect of our well-being as a nation. And never have the possible solutions had the potential to do so much good for so many generations to come.

Of course, many Americans have gotten this point, and it's true that the call for energy independence is now coming from an amazingly diverse coalition of interests. From farmers and businesses, military leaders and CIA officials, scientists and Evangelical Christians, auto executives and unions, and politicians of almost every political persuasion, people are realizing that an oil future is not a secure future for this country.

And yet, when it comes to finding a way to end our dependence on fossil fuels, the greatest vacuum in leadership, the biggest failure of imagination, and the most stubborn refusal to admit the need for change is coming from the very people who are running the country.

By now, the Bush Administration's record on climate change is almost legendary. This is the administration that commissioned government experts and scientists to do a study on global warming, only to omit the part from the final report that said it was caused by humans. This is the administration that didn't try to improve the Kyoto Treaty by trying to include oil guzzlers like

China and India, but walked away from the entire global effort to stem climate change. And just recently, this is the administration that tried to silence a NASA scientist for letting the rest of us know that, yes, climate change is a pretty big deal.

Meanwhile, it's pretty tough to make any real progress on this issue in Congress when the Chairman of the committee in charge of the environment thinks that, in the face of literally thousands of scientists and studies that say otherwise, global warming is the "greatest hoax ever perpetrated on the American people." And you know it's bad when the star witness at his global warming hearing is a science fiction writer.

Now, after the President's last State of the Union, when he told us that America was addicted to oil, there was a brief moment of hope that he'd finally do something on energy.

I was among the hopeful. But then I saw the plan.

His funding for renewable fuels is at the same level it was the day he took office. He refuses to call for even a modest increase in fuel-efficiency standards for cars. And his latest budget funds less then half of the energy bill he himself signed into law, leaving hundreds of millions of dollars in under-funded energy proposals.

This is not a serious effort. Saying that America is addicted to oil without following a real plan for energy independence is like admitting alcoholism and then skipping out on the 12-step program. It's not enough to identify the challenge—we have to meet it.

See, there's a reason that some have compared the quest for energy independence to the Manhattan Project or the Apollo moon landing. Like those historic efforts, moving away from an oil economy is a major challenge that will require a sustained national commitment.

During World War II, we had an entire country working around the clock to produce enough planes and tanks to beat the Axis powers. In the middle of the Cold War, we built a national highway system so we had a quick way to transport military equipment across the country. When we wanted to pull ahead of the Russians into space, we poured millions into a national education initiative that graduated thousands of new scientists and engineers.

America now finds itself at a similar crossroads. As gas prices keep rising, the Middle East grows ever more unstable, and the ice caps continue to melt, we face a now-or-never, once-in-a-generation opportunity to set this country on a different course.

Such a course is not only possible, it's already being pursued in other places around the world. Countries like Japan are creating jobs and slowing oil consumption by churning out and buying millions of fuel-efficient cars. Brazil, a nation that once relied on foreign countries to import eighty percent of its crude oil, will now be entirely self-sufficient in a few years thanks to its investment in biofuels.

So why can't we do this? Why can't we make energy security one of the great American projects of the 21st Century?

The answer is, with the right leadership, we can. We can do it by partnering with business, not fighting it. We can do it with technology we already have on the shelf. And we can do it by investing in the clean, cheap, renewable fuels that American farmers grow right here at home.

To deal directly with climate change, something we failed to do in the last energy bill, we should use a market-based strategy that gradually reduces harmful emissions in the most economical way. John McCain and Joe Lieberman are continuing to build support for legislation based on this approach, and Senators Bingaman and Domenici are also pursuing proposals that will cut carbon emissions. Right here in Chicago, the Chicago Climate Exchange is already running a legally binding greenhouse gas trading system.

The idea here is simple: if you're a business that can't yet meet the lower cap we'll put on harmful carbon emissions, you can either purchase credits from other companies that have achieved more than their emissions goal, or you can temporarily purchase a permit from the government, the money from which will go towards investments in clean energy technology. As Fred Krupp, the president of Environmental Defense has said, "Once you put a value on carbon reductions, you make winners out of innovators."

Any strategy for reducing carbon emissions must also deal with coal, which is actually the most abundant source of energy in this country. To keep using this fossil fuel, I believe we need to invest in the kind of advanced coal technology that will keep our air cleaner while still keeping our coal mines in business. Over the next two decades, power companies are expected to build dozens of new coal-fired power plants, and countries like India and China will build hundreds. If they use obsolete technology, these plants will emit over sixty billion tons of heat-trapping pollution into the atmosphere. We need to act now and make the United States a leader in putting in place the standards and incentives that will ensure that these plants use available technology to capture carbon dioxide and dispose of it safely underground.

But of course, one of the biggest contributors to our climate troubles and our energy dependence is oil, and so any plan for the future must drastically reduce our addiction to this dirty, dangerous, and ultimately finite source of energy.

We can do this by focusing on two things: the cars we drive and the fuels we use.

The President's energy proposal would reduce our oil imports by 4.5 million barrels per day by 2025. Not only can we do better than that, we must do better than that if we hope to make a real dent in our oil dependency. With technology we have on the shelves right now and fuels we can grow right here in America, by 2025 we can reduce our oil imports by over 7.5 million barrels per day, an amount greater than all the oil we are expected to import from the entire Middle East.

For years, we've hesitated to raise fuel economy standards as a nation in part because of a very legitimate concern—the impact it would have on Detroit. The auto industry is right when they argue that transitioning to more hybrid and fuel-efficient cars would require massive investment at a time when they're struggling under the weight of rising health care costs, sagging profits, and stiff competition.

But it's precisely because of that competition that they don't have a choice. China now has a higher fuel economy standard than we do, and Japan's Toyota is doubling production of the popular Prius to sell 100,000 in the U.S. this year.

There is now no doubt that fuel-efficient cars represent the future of the auto industry. If American car companies hope to be a part of that future—if they hope to survive—they must start building more of these cars. This isn't just about energy—this is about the ability to create millions of new jobs and save an entire American industry.

But that's not to say we should leave the industry to face the transition costs on its own. Yes, we should raise fuel economy standards by three percent a year over the next fifteen years, starting in 2008. With the technology they already have, this should be an achievable goal for automakers. But we can help them get there.

Right now, one of the biggest costs facing auto manufacturers isn't the cars they make; it's the health care they provide. Health care costs make up $1,500 of the price of every GM car that's made—more than the cost of steel. Retiree health care alone cost the Big Three automakers nearly $6.7 billion just last year.

I believe we should make the auto companies a deal that could solve this problem. It's a piece of legislation I introduced called "Health Care for Hybrids," and it would allow the federal government to pick up part of the tab for the auto companies' retiree health care costs. In exchange, the auto companies would then use some of that savings to build and invest in more fuel-efficient cars. It's a win-win proposal for the industry. Their retirees will be taken care of, they'll save money on health care, and they'll be free to invest in the kind of fuel-efficient cars that are the key to their competitive future.

But building cars that use less oil is only one side of the equation. The other involves replacing the oil we use with the home-grown biofuels that will finally slow the warming of the planet. In fact, one study shows that using cellulosic ethanol fuel instead of oil can reduce harmful emissions by up to seventy-five percent.

Already, there are hundreds of fueling stations that use a blend of ethanol and gasoline known as E85, and there are millions of cars on the road with the flexible-fuel tanks necessary to use this fuel, including my own right here in Illinois.

But the challenge we face with these biofuels is getting them out of the labs, out of the farms, and onto the wider commercial market.

The federal government can help in a few ways here, and recently, I introduced the "American Fuels Act" with Senator Dick Lugar to get us started.

First, this legislation would reduce the risk of investing in renewable fuels by providing loan guarantees and venture capital to those entrepreneurs with the best plans to develop and sell biofuels on a commercial market.

Second, it would let the private sector know that there will always be a market for renewable fuels by creating an alternative diesel standard in this country that would blend millions of more gallons of renewable fuels into the petroleum supply each year.

Third, it would help make sure that every single new car in America is a flexible-fuel vehicle within a decade. Currently it costs manufacturers just $100 to add these tanks to each car. But we can do them one better. If they install flexible-fuel tanks in their cars before the decade's up, we will provide them a $100 tax credit to do it, so there's no excuse for delay. And we'd also give consumers a bargain by offering a thirty-five cents tax credit for every gallon of E85 they use.

Fourth, this legislation calls for a Director of Energy Security to oversee all of our efforts. Like the Chairman of the Joint Chiefs and the National Intelligence Director, this person would be an advisor to the National Security Council and have the full authority to coordinate America's energy policy across all levels of government. He or she would approve all major budget decisions and provide a full report to Congress and the country every year detailing the progress we're making toward energy independence.

Finally, while it's not in the bill, we should also make sure that every single automobile the government purchases is a flexible-fuel vehicle—starting today. When it becomes possible in the coming years, we should also make sure that every government car is the type of hybrid that you can plug in to an outlet and recharge.

As the last few residents of Shishmaref pack up their homes and leave their tiny seaside village behind, I can't help but think that right now, history is testing our generation.

Will we let this happen all over the world? Will we stand by while drought and famine, storms and floods overtake our planet? Or will we look back at today and say that this was the moment when we took a stand? That this was the moment when we began to turn things around?

The climate changes we are experiencing are already causing us harm. But in the end, it will not be us who deal with its most devastating effects. It will be our children, and our grandchildren.

I have two daughters, aged three and seven. And I can't help but think that they are the reason I wanted to make a difference in this country in the first place—to give them a better, more hopeful world to raise their children.

This is our generation's chance to give them that world. It's a chance that will not last much longer, but if we work together and seize this moment, we can change the course of this nation forever. I hope we can start today.

THIS IS OUR TIME!
The "Take Back America" Speech
June 14, 2006

(Washington, D.C.) Barack Obama delivered this speech at the "Take Back America" Conference sponsored by the progressive Campaign For America's Future: *This is our time. Our time to make a mark on history. Our time to write a new chapter in the American story. Our time to leave our children a country that is freer and kinder, more prosperous and more just than the place we grew up.*

My friends, we meet here today at a time where we find ourselves at a crossroads in America's history.

It's a time where you can go to any town hall or street corner or coffee shop and hear people express the same anxiety about the future; hear them convey the same uncertainty about the direction we're headed as a country. Whether it's the war or Katrina or their health care or their jobs, you hear people say that we've finally arrived at a moment where something must change.

These are Americans who still believe in an America where anything's possible—they just don't think their leaders do. These are Americans who still dream big dreams—they just sense their leaders have forgotten how.

I remember when I first ran for the state Senate, my very first race. A seat had opened up, and some friends asked me if I'd be interested in running. Well, I thought about it, and then I did what every wise man does when faced with a difficult decision: I prayed, and I asked my wife.

And after consulting with these higher powers, I threw my hat in the ring and I did what every person on a campaign does: I talked to anyone who'd listen.

I went to bake sales and barber shops and if there were two guys standing on the corner I'd pull up and hand them literature. And everywhere I went I'd get two questions:

First, they'd ask, "Where'd you get that funny name, Barack Obama?" Because people just couldn't pronounce it. They'd call me "Alabama," or they'd call me "Yo Mama." And I'd have to explain that I got the name from my father, who was from Kenya.

And the second thing people would ask me was,

> "You seem like a nice young man. You teach law school, you're a civil rights attorney, you organize voter registration, you're a family man—why would you wanna go into something dirty and nasty like politics?"

And I understood the question because it revealed the cynicism people feel about public life today. That even though we may get involved out of civic obligation every few years, we don't always have confidence that government can make a difference in our lives.

So I understand the cynicism. But whenever I get in that mood, I think about something that happened to me on the eve of my election to the United States Senate.

We had held a large rally the night before in the Southside of Chicago, which is where I live. And in the midst of this rally, someone comes up to me and says that there's a woman who'd like to come meet you, and she's traveled a long way and she wants to take a picture and shake your hand.

And so I said fine, and I met her, and we talked.

And all of this would have been unremarkable except for the fact that this woman, Marguerite Lewis, was born in 1899 and was 105 years old.

And ever since I met this frail, one-hundred-and-five-year-old African-American woman who had found the strength to leave her house and come to a rally because she believed that her voice mattered, I've thought about all she's seen in her life.

I've thought about the fact that when she was born, there weren't cars on the road, and no airplanes in the sky. That she was born under the cloud of Jim Crow, free in theory but still enslaved in so many ways. That she was born at a time for black folks when lynchings were not uncommon, but voting was.

I've thought about how she lived to see a world war and a Great Depression and a second world war, and how she saw her brothers and uncles and nephews and cousins coming home from those wars and still have to sit at the back of a bus.

And I thought about how she saw women finally win the right to vote. And how she watched FDR lift this nation out of fear and send millions to college on the GI Bill and lift millions out of poverty with Social Security. How she saw unions rise up and a middle-class prosper, and watched immigrants leave distant shores in search of an idea known as America.

She believed in this idea with all her heart and she saw this progress around her and she had faith that someday it would be her turn. And when she finally saw hope breaking through the horizon in the Civil Rights Movement, she thought, "Maybe it's my turn."

And in that movement, she saw women who were willing to walk instead of ride the bus after a day of doing somebody else's laundry and looking after somebody else's children because they walked for freedom. And she saw young people of every race and every creed take a bus down to Mississippi and Alabama to register voters because they believed. She saw four little girls die in a Sunday school and catalyze a nation.

And at last—at last—she saw the passage of the Civil Rights Act and the Voting Rights Act.

And she saw people lining up to vote for the first time—and she got in that line—and she never forgot it. She kept on voting in each and every election because she believed. She believed that over a span of three centuries, she had seen enough to know that there is no challenge too great, no injustice too crippling, no destiny too far out of reach for America.

She believed that we don't have to settle for equality for some or opportunity for the lucky or freedom for the few.

And she knew that during those moments in history where it looked like we might give up hope or settle for less, there have always been Americans who refused. Who said we're going to keep on dreaming, and we're going to keep on building, and we're going to keep on marching, and we're going to keep on working because that's who we are. Because we've always fought to bring all of our people under the blanket of the American Dream.

And I think that we face one of those moments today.

In a century just six years old, our faith has been shaken by war and terror, disaster and despair, threats to the middle-class dream, and scandal and corruption in our government.

The sweeping changes brought by revolutions in technology have torn down walls between business and government and people and places all over the globe. And with this new world comes new risks and new dangers.

No longer can we assume that a high-school education is enough to compete for a job that could easily go to a college-educated student in Bangalore or Beijing. No more can we count on employers to provide health care and pensions and job training when their bottom-lines know no borders. Never again can we expect the oceans that surround America to keep us safe from attacks on our own soil.

The world has changed. And as a result, we've seen families work harder for less and our jobs go overseas. We've seen the cost of health care and child care and gasoline skyrocket. We've seen our children leave for Iraq and terrorists threaten to finish the job they started on 9/11.

But while the world has changed around us, too often our government has stood still. Our faith has been shaken, but the people running Washington aren't willing to make us believe again.

It's the timidity—the smallness—of our politics that's holding us back right now. The idea that some problems are just too big to handle, and if you just ignore them, sooner or later they'll go away.

That if you give a speech where you rattle off statistics about the stock market being up and orders for durable goods being on the rise, no one will notice the single mom whose two jobs won't pay the bills or the student who can't afford his college dreams.

That if you say the words "plan for victory" and point to the number of schools painted and roads paved and cell phones used in Iraq, no one will notice the nearly 2,500 flag-draped coffins that have arrived at Dover Air Force base.

Well it's time we finally said we notice, and we care, and we're not gonna settle anymore.

You know, you probably never thought you'd hear this at a Take Back America conference, but Newt Gingrich made a great point a few weeks ago. He was talking about what an awful job his own party has done governing this country, and he said that with all the mistakes and misjudgments the Republicans have made over the last six years, the slogan for the Democrats should come down to just two words: "Had enough?"

I don't know about you, but I think old Newt is onto something here. Because I think we've all had enough. Enough of the broken promises. Enough of the failed leadership. Enough of the can't-do, won't-do, won't-even-try style of governance.

Four years after 9/11, I've had enough of being told that we can find the money to give Paris Hilton more tax cuts, but we can't find enough to protect our ports or our railroads or our chemical plants or our borders.

I've had enough of the closed-door deals that give billions to the HMOs when we're told that we can't do a thing for the 45 million uninsured or the millions more who can't pay their medical bills.

I've had enough of being told that we can't afford body armor for our troops and health care for our veterans and benefits for the wounded heroes who've risked their lives for this country. I've had enough of that.

I've had enough of giving billions away to the oil companies when we're told that we can't invest in the renewable energy that will create jobs and lower gas prices and finally free us from our dependence on the oil wells of Saudi Arabia.

I've had enough of our kids going to schools where the rats outnumber the computers. I've had enough of Katrina survivors living out of their cars and begging FEMA for trailers. And I've had enough of being told that all we can do about this is sit and wait and hope that the good fortune of a few trickles on down to everyone else in this country.

You know, we all remember that George Bush said in the 2000 campaign that he was against nation-building. We just didn't know he was talking about this one.

Now, let me say this—I don't think that George Bush is a bad man. I think he loves his country. I don't think this administration is full of stupid people—I think there are a lot of smart folks in there. The problem isn't that their philosophy isn't working the way it's supposed to—it's that it is. It's that it's doing exactly what it's supposed to do.

The reason they don't believe government has a role in solving national problems is because they think government is the problem. That we're better off if we dismantle it—if we divvy it up into individual tax breaks, hand 'em out, and encourage everyone to go buy your own health care, your own retirement security, your own child care, their own schools, your own private security force, your own roads, their own levees.

It's called the Ownership Society in Washington. But in our past there has been another term for it—Social Darwinism—every man or women for him or herself.

It allows us to say to those whose health care or tuition may rise faster than they can afford—life isn't fair. It allows us to say to the child who didn't have the foresight to choose the right parents or be born in the right suburb—pick yourself up by your bootstraps. It lets us say to the guy who worked twenty or thirty years in the factory and then watched his plant move out to Mexico or China—we're sorry, but you're on your own.

It's a bracing idea. It's a tempting idea. And it's the easiest thing in the world.

But there's just one problem. It doesn't work. It ignores our history. Yes, our greatness as a nation has depended on individual initiative, on a belief in the free market. But it has also depended on our sense of mutual regard for each other, of mutual responsibility. The idea that everybody has a stake in the country, that we're all in it together and everybody's got a shot at opportunity.

Americans know this. We know that government can't solve all our problems—and we don't want it to.

But we also know that there are some things we can't do on our own. We know that there are some things we do better together.

We know that we've been called in churches and mosques, synagogues and Sunday schools to love our neighbors as ourselves, to be our brother's keeper, to be our sister's keeper. That we have individual responsibility, but we also have collective responsibility to each other.

85

That's what America is.

And so I am eager to have this argument not just with the President, but the entire Republican Party over what this country is about.

Because I think that this is our moment to lead.

The time for our party's identity crisis is over. Don't let anyone tell you we don't know what we stand for and don't doubt it yourselves. We know who we are. And in the end, we know that it isn't enough to just say that you've had enough.

So let it be said that we are the party of opportunity. That in a global economy that's more connected and more competitive, we are the party that will guarantee every American an affordable, world-class, top-notch, life-long education—from early childhood to high school, from college to on-the-job training.

Let it be said that we are the party of affordable, accessible health care for all Americans. The party that won't make Americans choose between a health care plan that bankrupts the government and one that bankrupts families. The party that won't just throw a few tax breaks at families who can't afford their insurance, but modernizes our health care system and gives every family a chance to buy insurance at a price they can afford.

Let it be said that we are the party of an energy independent America. The party that's not bought and paid for by the oil companies. The party that will harness homegrown, alternative fuels and spur the production of fuel-efficient, hybrid cars to break our dependence on the world's most dangerous regimes.

Let it be said that we will conduct a smart foreign policy that battles the forces of terrorism and fundamentalism wherever they may exist by matching the might of our military with the power of our diplomacy and the strength of our alliances. And when we do go to war, let us always be honest with the American people about why we are there and how we will win.

And let it be said that we are the party of open, honest government that doesn't peddle the agenda of whichever lobbyist or special interest can write the biggest check. The party who believes that, in this democracy, influence and access should begin and end with the power of the ballot.

If we do all this, if we can be trusted to lead, this will not be a Democratic agenda, it will be an American agenda. Because in the end, we may be proud Democrats, but we are prouder Americans. We're tired of being divided, tired of running into ideological walls and partisan roadblocks, tired of appeals to our worst instincts and greatest fears.

Americans everywhere are desperate for leadership. They are longing for direction. And they want to believe again.

A while ago, I was reading through Jonathan Kozol's new book, *Shame of a Nation*, which tells of his travels to underprivileged schools across America.

At one point, Kozol tells about his trip to Fremont High School in Los Angeles, where he met a girl who tells him that she'd taken hairdressing twice, because there were actually two different levels offered by the high school. The first was in hairstyling; the other in braiding.

Another girl, Mireya, listened as her friend told this story. And she began to cry. When asked what was wrong, she said, "I don't want to take hairdressing. I did not need sewing either. I knew how to sew. My mother is a seamstress in a factory. I'm trying to go to college. I don't need to sew to go to college. My mother sews. I hoped for something else."

I hoped for something else.

I've often thought about Mireya and her simple dream and all those before her who've shared that dream too.

And I've wondered—if she is lucky enough to live as long as 105-year-old Marguerite Lewis, if she someday has the chance to look back across the 21st Century, what will she see? Will she see a country that is freer and kinder, more tolerant and more just than the one she grew up in? Will she see greater opportunities for every citizen of this country? Will all her childhood hopes be fulfilled?

We are here tonight because we believe that in this country, we have it within our power to say "yes" to those questions, to forge our own destiny, to begin the world anew.

Ladies and gentlemen, this is our time.

Our time to make a mark on history.

Our time to write a new chapter in the American story.

Our time to leave our children a country that is freer and kinder, more prosperous and more just than the place we grew up.

And then someday, someday, if our kids get the chance to stand where we are and look back at the beginning of the 21st Century, they can say that this was the time when America renewed its purpose.

They can say that this was the time when America found its way.

They can say that this was the time when America learned to dream again.

POLITICS AND FAITH
A Call To Renewal
June 28, 2006

(Washington, D.C.) Barack Obama delivered the keynote speech at a conference sponsored by the evangelical anti-poverty group, Call To Renewal, taking as his theme the intersection of politics and faith: *Imagine Lincoln's Second Inaugural Address without reference to "the judgments of the Lord." Or King's I Have a Dream speech without references to "all of God's children." Their summoning of a higher truth helped inspire what had seemed impossible, and move the nation to embrace a common destiny.*

I appreciate the opportunity to speak here at the Call to Renewal's Building a Covenant for a New America conference. I've had the opportunity to take a look at your Covenant for a New America. It is filled with outstanding policies and prescriptions for much of what ails this country. So I'd like to congratulate you all on the thoughtful presentations you've given so far about poverty and justice in America, and for putting fire under the feet of the political leadership here in Washington.

But today I'd like to talk about the connection between religion and politics and perhaps offer some thoughts about how we can sort through some of the often bitter arguments that we've been seeing over the last several years.

I do so because, as you all know, we can affirm the importance of poverty in the Bible; and we can raise up and pass out this Covenant for a New America. We can talk to the press, and we can discuss the religious call to address poverty and environmental stewardship all we want—but it won't have an impact unless we tackle head-on the mutual suspicion that sometimes exists between religious America and secular America.

I want to give you an example that I think illustrates this fact. As some of you know, during the 2004 U.S. Senate General Election I ran against a gentleman named Alan Keyes. Mr. Keyes is well-versed in the Jerry Falwell-Pat Robertson style of rhetoric that often labels progressives as both immoral and godless.

Indeed, Mr. Keyes announced towards the end of the campaign that,

"Jesus Christ would not vote for Barack Obama. Christ would not vote for Barack Obama because Barack Obama has behaved in a way that it is inconceivable for Christ to have behaved."

Jesus Christ would not vote for Barack Obama.

Now, I was urged by some of my liberal supporters not to take this statement seriously, to essentially ignore it. To them, Mr. Keyes was an extremist, and his arguments not worth entertaining. And since at the time, I was up 40 points in the polls, it probably wasn't a bad piece of strategic advice.

But what they didn't understand, however, was that I had to take Mr. Keyes seriously, for he claimed to speak for my religion, and my God. He claimed knowledge of certain truths.

Mr. Obama says he's a Christian, he was saying, and yet he supports a lifestyle that the Bible calls an abomination.

Mr. Obama says he's a Christian, but supports the destruction of innocent and sacred life.

And so what would my supporters have me say? How should I respond? Should I say that a literalist reading of the Bible was folly? Should I say that Mr. Keyes, who is a Roman Catholic, should ignore the teachings of the Pope?

Unwilling to go there, I answered with what has come to be the typically liberal response in such debates, namely, I said that we live in a pluralistic society, that I can't impose my own religious views on another, that I was running to be the U.S. Senator of Illinois and not the Minister of Illinois.

But Mr. Keyes's implicit accusation that I was not a true Christian nagged at me, and I was also aware that my answer did not adequately address the role my faith has in guiding my own values and my own beliefs.

Now, my dilemma was by no means unique. In a way, it reflected the broader debate we've been having in this country for the last thirty years over the role of religion in politics.

For some time now, there has been plenty of talk among pundits and pollsters that the political divide in this country has fallen sharply along religious lines. Indeed, the single biggest "gap" in party affiliation among white Americans today is not between men and women, or those who reside in so-called red states and those who reside in blue, but between those who attend church regularly and those who don't.

Conservative leaders have been all too happy to exploit this gap, consistently reminding evangelical Christians that Democrats disrespect their values and dislike their Church, while suggesting to the rest of the country that religious Americans care only about issues like abortion and gay marriage; school prayer and intelligent design.

Democrats, for the most part, have taken the bait. At best, we may try to avoid the conversation about religious values altogether, fearful of offending anyone and claiming that, regardless of our personal beliefs, constitutional principles tie our hands. At worst, there are some liberals who dismiss religion in the public square as inherently irrational or intolerant, insisting on a caricature of religious Americans that paints them as fanatical, or thinking that the very word "Christian" describes one's political opponents, not people of faith.

Now, such strategies of avoidance may work for progressives when our opponent is Alan Keyes. But over the long haul, I think we make a mistake when we fail to acknowledge the power of faith in people's lives—in the lives of the American people—and I think it's time that we join a serious debate about how to reconcile faith with our modern, pluralistic democracy.

And if we're going to do that then we first need to understand that Americans are a religious people. Ninety percent of us believe in God, seventy percent affiliate themselves with an organized religion, thirty-eight percent call themselves committed Christians, and substantially more people in America believe in angels than they do in evolution.

This religious tendency is not simply the result of successful marketing by skilled preachers or the draw of popular mega-churches. In fact, it speaks to a hunger that's deeper than that—a hunger that goes beyond any particular issue or cause.

Each day, it seems, thousands of Americans are going about their daily rounds—dropping off the kids at school, driving to the office, flying to a business meeting, shopping at the mall, trying to stay on their diets—and they're coming to the realization that something is missing. They are deciding that their work, their possessions, their diversions, their sheer busyness, is not enough.

They want a sense of purpose, a narrative arc to their lives. They're looking to relieve a chronic loneliness, a feeling supported by a recent study that shows Americans have fewer close friends and confidants than ever before. And so they need an assurance that somebody out there cares about them, is listening to them, that they are not just destined to travel down that long highway towards nothingness.

And I speak with some experience on this matter. I was not raised in a particularly religious household, as undoubtedly many in the audience were. My father, who returned to Kenya when I was just two, was born Muslim but as an adult became an atheist. My mother, whose parents were non-practicing Baptists and Methodists, was probably one of the most spiritual and kindest people I've ever known, but grew up with a healthy skepticism of organized religion herself. As a consequence, so did I.

It wasn't until after college, when I went to Chicago to work as a community organizer for a group of Christian churches, that I confronted my own spiritual dilemma.

I was working with churches, and the Christians who I worked with recognized themselves in me. They saw that I knew their Book and that I shared their values and sang their songs. But they sensed that a part of me that remained removed, detached, that I was an observer in their midst.

And in time, I came to realize that something was missing as well—that without a vessel for my beliefs, without a commitment to a particular community of faith, at some level I would always remain apart, and alone.

And if it weren't for the particular attributes of the historically black church, I may have accepted this fate. But as the months passed in Chicago, I found myself drawn, not just to work with the church, but to be in the church.

For one thing, I believed and still believe in the power of the African-American religious tradition to spur social change, a power made real by some of the leaders here today. Because of its past, the black church understands in an intimate way the Biblical call to feed the hungry and cloth the naked and challenge powers and principalities. And in its historical struggles for freedom and the rights of man, I was able to see faith as more than just a comfort to the weary or a hedge against death, but rather as an active, palpable agent in the world. As a source of hope.

And perhaps it was out of this intimate knowledge of hardship—the grounding of faith in struggle—that the church offered me a second insight, one that I think is important to emphasize today.

Faith doesn't mean that you don't have doubts.

You need to come to church in the first place precisely because you are first of this world, not apart from it. You need to embrace Christ precisely because you have sins to wash away, because you are human and need an ally in this difficult journey.

It was because of these newfound understandings that I was finally able to walk down the aisle of Trinity United Church of Christ on 95th Street in the South Side of Chicago one day and affirm my Christian faith. It came about as a choice, and not an epiphany. I didn't fall out in church. The questions I had didn't magically disappear. But kneeling beneath that cross on the South Side, I felt that I heard God's spirit beckoning me. I submitted myself to His will, and dedicated myself to discovering His truth.

That's a path that has been shared by millions upon millions of Americans—evangelicals, Catholics, Protestants, Jews, and Muslims alike—some since birth, others at certain turning points in their lives. It is not something they set apart from the rest of their beliefs and values. In fact, it is often what drives their beliefs and their values.

And that is why that, if we truly hope to speak to people where they're at—to communicate our hopes and values in a way that's relevant to their own—then as progressives, we cannot abandon the field of religious discourse.

Because when we ignore the debate about what it means to be a good Christian or Muslim or Jew, when we discuss religion only in the negative sense of where or how it should not be practiced, rather than in the positive sense of what it tells us about our obligations towards one another; when we shy away from religious venues and religious broadcasts because we assume that we will be unwelcome—others will fill the vacuum, those with the most insular views of faith, or those who cynically use religion to justify partisan ends.

In other words, if we don't reach out to evangelical Christians and other religious Americans and tell them what we stand for, then the Jerry Falwells and Pat Robertsons and Alan Keyeses will continue to hold sway.

More fundamentally, the discomfort of some progressives with any hint of religion has often prevented us from effectively addressing issues in moral terms. Some of the problem here is rhetorical. If we scrub language of all religious content, we forfeit the imagery and terminology through which millions of Americans understand both their personal morality and social justice.

Imagine Lincoln's *Second Inaugural Address* without reference to "the judgments of the Lord." Or King's *I Have a Dream* speech without references to "all of God's children." Their summoning of a higher truth helped inspire what had seemed impossible, and move the nation to embrace a common destiny.

Our failure as progressives to tap into the moral underpinnings of the nation is not just rhetorical, though. Our fear of getting "preachy" may also lead us to discount the role that values and culture play in some of our most urgent social problems.

After all, the problems of poverty and racism, the uninsured and the unemployed, are not simply technical problems in search of the perfect ten point plan. They are rooted in both societal indifference and individual callousness, in the imperfections of man.

Solving these problems will require changes in government policy, but it will also require changes in hearts and a change in minds. I believe in keeping guns out of our inner cities, and that our leaders must say so in the face of the gun manufacturers' lobby. But I also believe that when a gang-banger shoots indiscriminately into a crowd because he feels somebody disrespected him, we've got a moral problem. There's a hole in that young man's heart—a hole that the government alone cannot fix.

I believe in vigorous enforcement of our non-discrimination laws. But I also believe that a transformation of conscience and a genuine commitment to diversity on the part of the nation's CEOs could bring about quicker results than a battalion of lawyers. They have more lawyers than us anyway.

I think that we should put more of our tax dollars into educating poor girls and boys. I think that the work that Marian Wright Edelman has done all her life is absolutely how we should prioritize our resources in the wealthiest nation on earth. I also think that we should give them the information about contraception that can prevent unwanted pregnancies, lower abortion rates, and help assure that that every child is loved and cherished.

But, you know, my Bible tells me that if we train a child in the way he should go, when he is old he will not turn from it. So I think faith and guidance can help fortify a young woman's sense of self, a young man's sense of responsibility, and a sense of reverence that all young people should have for the act of sexual intimacy.

I am not suggesting that every progressive suddenly latch on to religious terminology—that can be dangerous. Nothing is more transparent than inauthentic expressions of faith.... [S]ome politicians come and clap—off rhythm—to the choir. We don't need that.

In fact, because I do not believe that religious people have a monopoly on morality, I would rather have someone who is grounded in morality and ethics, and who is also secular, affirm their morality and ethics and values without pretending that they're something they're not. They don't need to do that. None of us need to do that.

But what I am suggesting is this—secularists are wrong when they ask believers to leave their religion at the door before entering into the public square. Frederick Douglas, Abraham Lincoln, Williams Jennings Bryant, Dorothy Day, Martin Luther King— indeed, the majority of great reformers in American history— were not only motivated by faith, but repeatedly used religious language to argue for their cause. So to say that men and women should not inject their "personal morality" into public policy debates is a practical absurdity. Our law is by definition a codification of morality, much of it grounded in the Judeo-Christian tradition.

Moreover, if we progressives shed some of these biases, we might recognize some overlapping values that both religious and secular people share when it comes to the moral and material direction of our country. We might recognize that the call to sacrifice on behalf of the next generation, the need to think in terms of "thou" and not just "I," resonates in religious congregations all across the country. And we might realize that we have the ability to reach out to the evangelical community and engage millions of religious Americans in the larger project of American renewal.

Some of this is already beginning to happen. Pastors ... are wielding their enormous influences to confront AIDS, Third World debt relief, and the genocide in Darfur. Religious thinkers and activists ... are lifting up the Biblical injunction to help the poor as a means of mobilizing Christians against budget cuts to social programs and growing inequality.

And by the way, we need Christians on Capitol Hill, Jews on Capitol Hill, and Muslims on Capitol Hill, talking about the estate tax. When you've got an estate tax debate that proposes a trillion dollars being taken out of social programs to go to a handful of folks who don't need and weren't even asking for it, you know that we need an injection of morality in our political debate.

Across the country, individual churches like my own and your own are sponsoring day care programs, building senior centers, helping ex-offenders reclaim their lives, and rebuilding our gulf coast in the aftermath of Hurricane Katrina.

So the question is, how do we build on these still-tentative partnerships between religious and secular people of good will? It's going to take more work, a lot more work than we've done so far. The tensions and the suspicions on each side of the religious divide will have to be squarely addressed. And each side will need to accept some ground rules for collaboration.

While I've already laid out some of the work that progressive leaders need to do, I want to talk a little bit about what conservative leaders need to do, some truths they need to acknowledge.

For one, they need to understand the critical role that the separation of church and state has played in preserving not only our democracy, but the robustness of our religious practice. Folks tend to forget that during our founding, it wasn't the atheists or the civil libertarians who were the most effective champions of the First Amendment. It was the persecuted minorities, it was Baptists like John Leland who didn't want the established churches to impose their views on folks who were getting happy out in the fields and teaching the scripture to slaves. It was the forbearers of the evangelicals who were the most adamant about not mingling government with religious, because they did not want state-sponsored religion hindering their ability to practice their faith as they understood it.

Moreover, given the increasing diversity of America's population, the dangers of sectarianism have never been greater. Whatever we once were, we are no longer just a Christian nation; we are also a Jewish nation, a Muslim nation, a Buddhist nation, a Hindu nation, and a nation of nonbelievers.

And even if we did have only Christians in our midst—if we expelled every non-Christian from the United States of America—whose Christianity would we teach in the schools? Would we go with James Dobson's, or Al Sharpton's? Which passages of Scripture should guide our public policy? Should we go with Leviticus, which suggests slavery is okay and that eating shellfish is abomination? How about Deuteronomy, which suggests stoning your child if he strays from the faith? Or should we just stick to the Sermon on the Mount, a passage that is so radical that it's doubtful that our own Defense Department would survive its application? So before we get carried away, let's read our bibles. Folks haven't been reading their bibles.

This brings me to my second point. Democracy demands that the religiously motivated translate their concerns into universal, rather than religion-specific, values. It requires that their proposals be subject to argument, and amenable to reason. I may be opposed to abortion for religious reasons, but if I seek to pass a law banning the practice, I cannot simply point to the teachings of my church or evoke God's will. I have to explain why abortion violates some principle that is accessible to people of all faiths, including those with no faith at all.

Now this is going to be difficult for some who believe in the inerrancy of the Bible, as many evangelicals do. But in a pluralistic democracy, we have no choice. Politics depends on our ability to persuade each other of common aims based on a common reality. It involves the compromise, the art of what's possible. At some fundamental level, religion does not allow for compromise. It's the art of the impossible. If God has spoken, then followers are expected to live up to God's edicts, regardless of the consequences. To base one's life on such uncompromising commitments may be sublime, but to base our policy making on such commitments would be a dangerous thing. And if you doubt that, let me give you an example.

We all know the story of Abraham and Isaac. Abraham is ordered by God to offer up his only son, and without argument, he takes Isaac to the mountaintop, binds him to an altar, and raises his knife, prepared to act as God has commanded.

Of course, in the end God sends down an angel to intercede at the very last minute, and Abraham passes God's test of devotion.

But it's fair to say that if any of us leaving this church saw Abraham on a roof of a building raising his knife, we would, at the very least, call the police and expect the Department of Children and Family Services to take Isaac away from Abraham. We would do so because we do not hear what Abraham hears, do not see what Abraham sees, true as those experiences may be. So the best we can do is act in accordance with those things that we all see, and that we all hear, be it common laws or basic reason.

Finally, any reconciliation between faith and democratic pluralism requires some sense of proportion.

This goes for both sides.

Even those who claim the Bible's inerrancy make distinctions between Scriptural edicts, sensing that some passages—the Ten Commandments, say, or a belief in Christ's divinity—are central to Christian faith, while others are more culturally specific and may be modified to accommodate modern life.

The American people intuitively understand this, which is why the majority of Catholics practice birth control and some of those opposed to gay marriage nevertheless are opposed to a Constitutional amendment to ban it. Religious leadership need not accept such wisdom in counseling their flocks, but they should recognize this wisdom in their politics.

But a sense of proportion should also guide those who police the boundaries between church and state. Not every mention of God in public is a breach to the wall of separation. Context matters. It is doubtful that children reciting the Pledge of Allegiance feel oppressed or brainwashed as a consequence of muttering the phrase "under God." I didn't. Having voluntary student prayer groups use school property to meet should not be a threat, any more than its use by the High School Republicans should threaten Democrats. And one can envision certain faith-based programs—targeting ex-offenders or substance abusers—that offer a uniquely powerful way of solving problems.

So we all have some work to do here. But I am hopeful that we can bridge the gaps that exist and overcome the prejudices each of us bring to this debate. And I have faith that millions of believing Americans want that to happen. No matter how religious they may or may not be, people are tired of seeing faith used as a tool of attack. They don't want faith used to belittle or to divide. They're tired of hearing folks deliver more screed than sermon. Because in the end, that's not how they think about faith in their own lives.

So let me end with just one other interaction I had during my campaign. A few days after I won the Democratic nomination in my U.S. Senate race, I received an e-mail from a doctor at the University of Chicago Medical School that said the following:

> "Congratulations on your overwhelming and inspiring primary win. I was happy to vote for you, and I will tell you that I am seriously considering voting for you in the general election. I write to express my concerns that may, in the end, prevent me from supporting you."

The doctor described himself as a Christian who understood his commitments to be "totalizing." His faith led him to a strong opposition to abortion and gay marriage, although he said that his faith also led him to question the idolatry of the free market and quick resort to militarism that seemed to characterize much of the Republican agenda.

But the reason the doctor was considering not voting for me was not simply my position on abortion. Rather, he had read an entry that my campaign had posted on my website, which suggested that I would fight "right-wing ideologues who want to take away a woman's right to choose." The doctor went on to write,

> "I sense that you have a strong sense of justice, and I also sense that you are a fair-minded person with a high regard for reason. Whatever your convictions, if you truly believe that those who oppose abortion are all ideologues driven by per-

verse desires to inflict suffering on women, then you, in my judgment, are not fair-minded. You know that we enter times that are fraught with possibilities for good and for harm, times when we are struggling to make sense of a common polity in the context of plurality, when we are unsure of what grounds we have for making any claims that involve others. I do not ask at this point that you oppose abortion, only that you speak about this issue in fair-minded words."

Fair-minded words.

So I looked at my website and found the offending words. In fairness to them, my staff had written them using standard Democratic boilerplate language to summarize my pro-choice position during the Democratic primary, at a time when some of my opponents were questioning my commitment to protect *Roe v. Wade*.

Re-reading the doctor's letter, though, I felt a pang of shame. It is people like him who are looking for a deeper, fuller conversation about religion in this country. They may not change their positions, but they are willing to listen and learn from those who are willing to speak in fair-minded words. Those who know of the central and awesome place that God holds in the lives of so many, and who refuse to treat faith as simply another political issue with which to score points.

So I wrote back to the doctor, and I thanked him for his advice. The next day, I circulated the e-mail to my staff and changed the language on my website to state in clear but simple terms my pro-choice position. And that night, before I went to bed, I said a prayer of my own—a prayer that I might extend the same presumption of good faith to others that the doctor had extended to me.

.... It's a prayer I think I share with a lot of Americans. A hope that we can live with one another in a way that reconciles the beliefs of each with the good of all. It's a prayer worth praying, and a conversation worth having in this country in the months and years to come.

EMBRYONIC STEM CELL RESEARCH
A Speech To The United States Senate
July 17, 2006

(Washington, D.C.) Barack Obama delivered this speech to the U.S. Senate in support of federal funding for embryonic stem cell research: *For most of our history, medicine has offered little hope of recovery to individuals affected by these and other devastating illnesses and injuries. Until now.*

A few weeks ago I was visited by two of my constituents—Mary Schneider and her son Ryan.

When Ryan was just two years old, his parents and doctors noted severe delays in his motor and speech development, and he was diagnosed with cerebral palsy. His parents were devastated, as the prognosis for many children with cerebral palsy is quite grim, and given the severity of Ryan's condition, his doctors didn't have much hope for his improvement.

Yet, his parents had hope. Because, when Ryan was born, his parents had saved his cord blood, a viable but limited source of stem cells. They found a doctor at Duke University who was willing to perform an experimental infusion with these cells to see if they might improve his condition.

They did. In fact, they seem to have cured him.

Within months of the infusion, Ryan was able to speak, use his arms, and eat normally, just like any other child—a miracle his family had once only dreamed of.

Ryan's story exemplifies the power and the promise of stem cells to treat and cure the millions of Americans who are suffering from catastrophic, debilitating, and life-threatening diseases and health conditions.

Each year, 100,000 Americans will develop Alzheimer's disease. Over 1 million adults will be diagnosed with diabetes this year, which can lead to complications such as blindness, damaged nerves, and loss of kidney function. And there are far too many individuals with spinal cord injuries who are struggling to maintain mobility and independence.

For most of our history, medicine has offered little hope of recovery to individuals affected by these and other devastating illnesses and injuries.

Until now.

Recent developments in stem cell research may hold the key to improved treatments, if not cures, for those affected by Alzheimer's disease, diabetes, spinal cord injury and countless other conditions.

Many men, women, and children who are cancer survivors are already familiar with the life-saving applications of adult stem cell research. Patients with leukemia or lymphoma often undergo bone marrow transplants, a type of stem cell transplant, which can significantly prolong life, or permanently get rid of the cancer. This therapy has been used successfully for decades, and is saving lives everyday.

Yet this breakthrough has its serious limitations. Adult stem cells, such as those used in bone marrow transplants, can only be collected in small quantities, may not be a match for the patient, and have limited ability to transform into specialized cells.

Cord blood, like the kind Ryan used, has limitations as well. If, for example, young Ryan's condition should deteriorate or he should develop another illness, there simply are not enough cord blood cells left for a second use.

His mother has told us that the few remaining cells would have to be cloned to get enough cells for future use, or they would have to obtain stem cells from another source.

These and other difficulties are the reasons why scientists have started to explore other types and other sources for stem cells, including embryonic stem cell research.

Embryonic stem cells can be obtained from a number of sources, including in vitro fertilization. At this very moment, there are over 400,000 embryos being stored in over four hundred facilities throughout the United States. The majority of these are reserved for infertile couples. However, many of these embryos will go unused, destined for permanent storage in a freezer or disposal. We should expand and accelerate research using these embryos, just as we should continue to explore the viability of adult stem cell use and cord blood use.

All over the country, exciting progress is being made in the area of embryonic stem cell research. At the University of Illinois, they're finding that stem cells have the potential to treat blood disorders, lung diseases, and heart damage.

At Johns Hopkins, researchers were able to use mouse embryonic stem cells to repair damaged nerves and restore mobility in paralyzed rats. One can't help but think that it's a matter of when, not if, this research will be able to one day help those who have lost the ability to walk.

For these reasons, I'm proud to be a long-term supporter of greater stem cell research. While I was a member of the Illinois Senate, I was the chief co-sponsor of the Ronald Reagan Biomedical Research Act, which would specifically permit embryonic stem cell research in Illinois, and establish review of this research by the Illinois Department of Public Health.

And I'm proud to be a co-sponsor of the stem cell bill before us today. This bill embodies the innovative thinking that we as a society demand and medical advancement requires. By expanding scientific access to embryonic stem cells which would be otherwise discarded, this bill will help our nation's scientists and researchers develop treatments and cures to help people who suffer from illnesses and injuries for which there are currently none. But the bill is not without limits; it requires that scientific research also be subject to rigorous oversight.

I realize there are moral and ethical issues surrounding this debate. But I also realize that we're not talking about harvesting cells that would've been used to create life and we're not talking about cloning humans. We're talking about using stem cells that would have otherwise been discarded and lost forever—and we're talking about using those stem cells to possibly save the lives of millions of Americans.

Democrats want this bill to pass. Conservative, pro-life Republicans want this bill to pass. By large margins, the American people want this bill to pass. It is only the White House standing in the way of progress—standing in the way of so many potential cures.

I would only ask that the President thinks about this before he picks up his pen to deliver his first veto in six years. I would ask that he thinks about Ryan Schneider and his parents, and all the other families who are sitting and waiting and praying for a cure, hoping that somewhere a researcher or scientist will find the answer.

There was a time in the middle of the last century when America watched helplessly as a mysterious disease left thousands—especially children—disabled for life. The medical community worked tirelessly to try and find a cure, but they needed help—they needed funding to make their research possible.

With a world war raging and the country still emerging from depression, the federal government could have ignored their plight or told them to find a cure on their own.

But that didn't happen. Instead, Franklin Delano Roosevelt helped galvanize a community of compassion and organize the March of Dimes to find the cure for polio. And while Roosevelt knew that his own polio would never be cured by the discovery of a vaccine, he also knew that, at its best, government can be used as a force to accomplish together what we cannot achieve on our own.

And so the people began to care and the dimes piled up and the funding started to flow, and fifty years ago, Jonas Salk discovered the polio vaccine.

Americans are looking for that kind of leadership today. All over the country, patients and their families are waiting today for Congress and the President to open the door to the cures of tomorrow. At the dawn of the 21st Century, we should approach this research with the same passion and commitment that have led to so many cures and saved so many lives throughout our history.

THE VOTING RIGHTS ACT
A Speech To The United States Senate
July 20, 2006

(Washington, D.C.) Barack Obama delivered this speech on the floor of the U.S. Senate in support of the reauthorization of the historic 1965 Voting Rights Act: *The Voting Rights Act has been a critical tool in ensuring that all Americans not only have the right to vote, but the right to have their vote counted.*

I rise today, both humbled and honored by the opportunity to express my support for renewal of the expiring provisions of the Voting Rights Act of 1965.

I want to thank the many people inside and outside of Congress who worked so hard over the past year to get us here....

And I want to thank both chambers, and both sides of the aisle, for getting this done with the same broad support that drove the original Act forty years ago. At a time when Americans are frustrated with the partisan bickering that too often stalls our work, the refreshing display of bipartisanship we are seeing today reflects our collective belief in the success of the Act and reminds us of how effective we can be when we work together.

Nobody can deny that we've come a long way since 1965.

Look at registration numbers. Only two years after passage of the original Act, registration numbers for minority voters in some states doubled. Soon after, not a single state covered by the Voting Rights Act had registered less than half of its minority voting-age population.

Look at the influence of African-American elected officials at all levels of government. There are African-American members of Congress. Since 2001, our nation's top diplomat has been an African-American.

In fact, most of America's elected African-American officials come from the states covered by Section 5 of the Voting Rights Act—states like Mississippi and Alabama and Louisiana and Georgia.

But to me the most striking evidence of our progress can be found right across this building, in my dear friend, Congressman John Lewis, who was on the front lines of the civil rights movement, risking life and limb for freedom. And on March 7, 1965, he led six hundred peaceful protestors demanding the right to vote across the Edmund Pettus Bridge in Selma, Alabama.

I've often thought about the people on the Edmund Pettus Bridge that day. Not only John Lewis and Hosea Williams leading the march, but the hundreds of everyday Americans who left their homes and their churches to join it. Blacks and whites, teenagers and children, teachers and bankers and shopkeepers—a beloved community of God's children ready to stand for freedom.

And I wonder, where did they find that kind of courage? When you're facing row after row of state troopers on horseback armed with billy clubs and tear gas, when they're coming toward you spewing hatred and violence, how do you simply stop, kneel down, and pray to the Lord for salvation?

But the most amazing thing of all is that after that day—after John Lewis was beaten within an inch of his life, after people's heads were gashed open and their eyes were burned and they watched their children's innocence literally beaten out of them—after all that, they went back to march again.

They marched again. They crossed the bridge. They awakened a nation's conscience, and not five months later, the Voting Rights Act of 1965 was signed into law. And it was reauthorized in 1970, 1975, and 1982.

Now, in 2006, John Lewis, the physical scars from those marches still visible, is an original cosponsor of the fourth reauthorization of the Voting Rights Act, and he was joined last week by 389 of his House colleagues in voting for its passage.

There are some who argue the Act is no longer needed, that the protections of Section 5's "pre-clearance" requirement—a requirement that ensures certain states are upholding the right to vote—are targeting the wrong states. But the evidence refutes that notion. Of the 1,100 objections issued by the Department of Justice since 1965, fifty-six percent occurred since the last reauthorization in 1982. So, despite the progress these states have made in upholding the right to vote, it's clear that problems still exist.

Others have argued against renewing Section 203's protection of language minorities. Unfortunately, these arguments have been tied to the debate over immigration and muddle a non-controversial issue—protecting the right to vote—with one of today's most contentious debates.

But let's remember: you can't request language assistance if you're not a voter, and you can't be a voter if you're not a citizen. And while voters, as citizens, must be proficient in English, many are simply more confident that they can cast ballots printed in their native languages without making errors.

A representative of the Southwestern Voter Registration Project is quoted as saying: "Citizens who prefer Spanish registration cards do so because they feel more connected to the process; they also feel they trust the process more when they understand it." These sentiments—connection to and trust in our democratic process—are exactly what we want from our voting rights legislation.

Our challenges don't end at reauthorizing the Voting Rights Act either. We have to prevent the problems we've seen in recent elections from happening again. We've seen political operatives purge voters from registration rolls for no legitimate reason, prevent eligible ex-felons from casting ballots, distribute polling equipment unevenly, and deceive voters about the time, location and rules of elections. Unfortunately, these efforts have been directed primarily at minorities, the disabled, low-income individuals, and other historically disenfranchised groups.

The Help America Vote Act was a big step in the right direction, but we need to do more. We need to fully fund HAVA. We need to enforce critical requirements like statewide registration databases. We need to make sure polling equipment is distributed equitably and that the equipment works. And we need to work on getting more people to the polls on election day.

We need to make sure that minority voters are not the subject of deplorable intimidation tactics when they do get to the polls. In 2004, Native American voters in South Dakota were confronted by men posing as law enforcement. These hired intimidators joked about jail time for ballot missteps, and followed voters to their cars to record their license plate numbers.

In Lake County, Ohio, some voters received a memo on bogus Board of Elections letterhead informing voters who registered through Democratic and NAACP drives that they could not vote.

In Wisconsin, a flier purporting to be from the "Milwaukee Black Voters League" was circulated in predominantly African-American neighborhoods with the following message:

> "If you've already voted in any election this year, you can't vote in the presidential election. If you violate any of these laws, you can get ten years in prison and your children will get taken away from you."

So, we have much more work to do. This occasion is cause for celebration, but it's also an opportunity to renew our commitment to voting rights. As Congressman Lewis said last week, "It's clear that we have come a great distance, but we still have a great distance to go."

The memory of Selma still lives on in the spirit of the Voting Rights Act. Since that day, the Voting Rights Act has been a critical tool in ensuring that all Americans not only have the right to vote, but the right to have their vote counted. Those of us concerned about protecting those rights can't afford to sit on our laurels upon reauthorization of this bill. We must take advantage of this rare united front and continue the fight to ensure unimpeded access to the polls for all Americans. In other words, we need to take the spirit that existed on that bridge, and we have to spread it across this country.

Two weeks after the first march was turned back, Dr. King told a gathering of organizers and activists and community members that they should not despair because the arc of the moral universe is long, but it bends towards justice. That's because of the work that each of us do to bend it towards justice. It's because of people like John Lewis and Fannie Lou Hamer and Coretta Scott King and Rosa Parks, all the giants upon whose shoulders we stand, that we are the beneficiaries of that arc bending towards justice.

That's why I stand here today. I would not be in the United States Senate had it not been for the efforts and courage of so many parents and grandparents and ordinary people who were willing to reach up and bend that arc in the direction of justice. I hope we continue to see that spirit live on, not just during this debate, but throughout all our work here in the Senate.

THE KATRINA GRADUATES
Commencement Address at Xavier University
Friday, August 11, 2006

(New Orleans, Louisiana) Barack Obama delivered this Commencement Address at Xavier University, taking as his theme the students' survival of Hurricane Katrina: *Katrina may well be the most dramatic test you face in life, but it will by no means be the last.*

I want to start by thanking you all for allowing me to share in your miracle today. Over the past year there has been no shortage of doubts about whether this college would live to see another commencement—and doubts remain still about the future of this great city. But on this summer's day in New Orleans, less than one year after the worst storm in American history beat down your door, I look out at the largest class to ever graduate from this college and know that one thing is certain—Xavier University is back.

I have to say that I'm pretty humbled to be here. Each year there are hundreds of commencements in this country. All are hopeful, some are inspiring, and most of you probably won't even remember who your speaker was ten years from now. As a rule, they usually involve an old guy like me giving young folks like you advice about what to expect in the real world—advice about the challenges you'll face and the obstacles you'll have to overcome.

But this is different. In the last month, I have walked among New Orleans' battered homes and empty streets and scattered debris that prove armies aren't the only ones who can wage wars on cities. I have seen pictures of Xavier after the storm—the submerged classrooms and the shattered windows and the dorm rooms that were left with books sitting open on desks and clothes still unpacked on the bed. And I have heard the story of nearly four hundred students and faculty who were trapped on campus in the days after Katrina, waiting on the roof to be rescued, with a sign that simply read "Help Us."

And as I thought about all of this, it dawned on me that when it comes to giving advice about challenges and obstacles, it's you who could probably teach the rest of us a thing or two about what it takes to overcome.

I could give you a lecture on courage, but some of you know what it is to wait huddled in the dark without electricity or running water, wondering if a helicopter or boat will come for you before the gunshots get closer or the food runs out or the waters rise.

I could talk at length about perseverance, but this is a class that was forced to scatter to schools across the country at the beginning of your senior year, leaving everything you knew behind while you waited to find out if you could ever come back.

And I could go on and on about the importance of community—about what it means to care for each other—but this is a school where so many sacrificed so much in order to open your doors in January—a triumph that showed the rest of America that there are those who refuse to desert this city and its people no matter what.

Yours has been an education that cannot simply be measured in the tests you've taken or the diploma you're about to receive. For it has also been an education in humanity, brought about by a force of nature—a lesson in both our capacity for good and in the imperfections of man, in our ability to rise to great challenges and our tendency to sometimes fall short of our obligations to one another.

Some will take an entire lifetime to experience these lessons—others never will. But as some of Katrina's youngest survivors, you've had a front row seat.

So what does this mean for you?

Well, lessons can be just as easily unlearned as they are learned. Time may heal, but it can also cloud the memory and remove us further from that initial core of concern.

And so what this all means is that, today and every day, you have a responsibility to remember what happened here in New Orleans. To make it a part of who you are. To let its lessons guide you as face your own challenges.

After all, Katrina may well be the most dramatic test you face in life, but it will by no means be the last. There will be quiet tests of character—the shoulder you lend a friend during their time of need, the way you raise your children, the care you give a loved one who's sick or dying, the integrity and honesty with which you carry yourself.

There will be powerful personal tests—the profession you choose, the legacy you leave, your ability to handle failure and disappointment.

And of course, there are the tests you will face as citizen—whether you use your voice to rage against injustice, whether you use your time to give back to your community, whether you use your passion to commit yourself to a cause larger than yourself.

In most of these tests, there are two different paths you can take.

One is easy. After graduating from a great school like Xavier, you'll pretty much be able to punch your own ticket, which means you can take your diploma, walk off this stage, leave this city, and go chasing after the big house and the large salary and the nice suits and all the other things that our money culture says you should buy.

You can live in neighborhoods with people who are exactly like yourself, and send your kids to the same schools, and narrow your concerns to what's going in your own little circle.

And when you turn on the TV or open the newspaper and hear about all the trouble in the world, there will be pundits and politicians who'll tell you that it's someone else's fault and someone else's problem to fix.

They'll tell you that the Americans who sleep in the streets and beg for food got there because they're all lazy or weak of spirit. That the immigrants who risk their lives to cross a desert have nothing to contribute to this country and no desire to embrace our ideals. That the inner-city children who are trapped in dilapidated schools can't learn and won't learn and so we should just give up on them entirely. That the innocent people being slaughtered and expelled from their homes in Darfur are somebody else's problem to take care of.

And when you hear all this, the easiest thing in the world will be to do nothing at all. To turn off the TV, put down the paper, and walk away from the stories about Iraq or poverty or violence or joblessness or hopelessness. To go about your busy lives, to remain detached, to remain indifferent, to remain safe.

But if you should ever think about taking this path, I ask you first to remember.

Remember witnessing the pain that neglect and indifference can cause—how entire neighborhoods in this city were left to drown because no one thought to make sure that every person had the means to escape. Remember what happens when responsibilities are ignored and bucks are passed—when the White House blames FEMA and FEMA blames the state of Louisiana and pretty soon no one's fixing the problem because everyone thought somebody else would. And whenever you're tempted to view the poor or the ill or the persecuted as "those people"—people in their own world with their own problems—remember always your neighbors in places like the Ninth Ward—men and women and children who, just like you, wanted desperately to escape to somewhere better.

And if you remember all of this—if you remember what happened here in New Orleans, if you allow it to change you forever—know that there is another path you can take.

This one is more difficult. It asks more of you. It asks you to leave here and not just pursue your own individual dreams, but to help perfect our collective dream as a nation. It asks you to realize there is more to life than being rich, thin, young, famous, safe, and entertained. It asks you to recognize that there are people out there who need you.

You know, there's a lot of talk in this country about the federal deficit. But I think we should talk more about our empathy deficit—the ability to put ourselves in someone else's shoes, to see the world through the eyes of those who are different from us—the child who's hungry, the steelworker who's been laid off, the family who lost the entire life they built together when the storm came to town.

When you think like this—when you choose to broaden your ambit of concern and empathize with the plight of others, whether they are close friends or distant strangers—it becomes harder not to act, harder not to help.

For each of you, this desire to do for others and serve your communities will come even easier if you allow yourself to remember what you saw here in New Orleans.

Because aside from all the bad that came from Katrina—the failures and the neglect, the incompetence and the apathy—you were also witness to a good that many forgot was even possible.

You saw people from every corner of this country drop what they were doing, leave their homes, and come to New Orleans—Americans who didn't know a soul in the entire city, who found their own piece of driftwood, built their own make-shift raft, and waded through the streets of this city, saving anyone they could. You saw the doctors and the nurses who refused to leave their city and their patients even when they were told time and again by local officials that it was no longer safe, even when helicopters were waiting to take them away. Men and women who stayed to care for the sick and dying long after their medical equipment and electricity were gone.

And after the storm had passed, you saw a spirit of generosity that spanned an entire globe, with billions upon billions in donations coming from tiny, far-off nations like Qatar and Sri Lanka. Think about that. These are places a lot of folks couldn't even identify on a map. Sri Lanka was still recovering from the devastation caused by last year's tsunami. And yet, they heard about our tragedy, and they gave.

Remember always this goodness. Remember always that while many in Washington and on all levels of government failed New Orleans, there were plenty of ordinary people who displayed extraordinary humanity during this city's hour of need.

In the years to come, return this favor to those who are forced to weather their own storms, be it the loss of a job or a slide into poverty, an unexpected illness or an unforeseen eviction. And in returning these favors, seek also to make this a nation of no more Katrinas. Make this a nation where we never again leave behind any American by ensuring that every American has a job that can support a family, and health care in case they get sick, and a good education for their child, and a secure retirement they can count on. Make this a nation where we are never again caught unprepared to meet the challenges of our time, where we free ourselves from a dependence on oil and protect our cities from both forces of terror and nature.

Make this a nation that is worthy of the sacrifices of so many of its citizens, and in doing so, make real the observation made by a visitor to our country so many centuries ago: "America is great because Americans are good."

I ask you to take this second path—this harder path—not because you have an obligation to those who are less fortunate, although you do have that obligation. Not because you have a debt to all of those who helped you get to where you are, although you do have that debt.

I ask you to take it because you have an obligation to yourself. Because our individual salvation depends on our collective salvation. And because it's only when you hitch your wagon to something larger than yourself that you will realize your true potential.

It is said that faith is a belief in things not seen, and miracles, by their nature, are inexplicable gifts from God.

But sometimes, if we look hard enough at the moments we triumph against the greatest of odds, we can see His will at work in the people He loves.

It's now well-known in this community that when your President, Norman Francis, promised to re-open this school by January, he joked that his decision would be recorded by history as either "crazy and stupid" or "bold and visionary."

And when I heard that, I wondered where you find the courage to make such a crazy, visionary promise, and where you find the commitment to keep it.

And I thought, Norman Francis is someone who remembers—remembers where he came from, remembers the lessons he learned, remembers the opportunities he's had, and lives his life according to those memories.

Born in Lafayette before Civil Rights and Voting Rights were even a possibility, this is a man who was raised in poverty, earning extra money for his parents as a child by shining shoes. He studied hard through high school, put himself through Xavier by working long hours in the library, and became the first ever African-American to be accepted into Loyola's Law School.

He graduated that law school and could've gone anywhere and made any amount of money, but Norman Francis wanted to help people learn because he remembered all the people who helped him.

And so he came back to Xavier, and he worked his way up through the ranks, and he became the first ever African-American president of this school at just thirty-six years old.

Since that day he has had many accolades and many chances to do whatever he wished with his life. He has been an advisor to four U.S. Presidents, served on a commission to the Vatican, and as President of the United Negro College Fund.

But through all of this, he decided to stay here in New Orleans, and build this university.

And so when Katrina tried to tear it down, you can understand why he refused to let that happen, why he put aside tending to the damage in his own house so that he could work on rebuilding this one, why he believed more than anything in his promise that these doors would open in January.

Norman Francis has helped make today's miracle because he has seen miracles at work in his own life. Now that you have seen one in yours, it's your turn to live a life committed to others, devoted to the impossible, and ever aware of the lessons you learned in New Orleans.

I've noticed that in the rebuilding effort throughout this city, one of the last things to come back, and yet the easiest to notice, is the greenery that makes any community seem alive. And as I saw a newly planted tree on my last trip here, I thought of a passage from the book of Job: "There is hope for a tree if it be cut down that it will sprout again, and that its tender branch will not cease."

Katrina was not the end of the tough times for New Orleans, and you will continue to face your own tests and challenges in the years to come. But if someone were to ask me how the tree stands on this August day, I would tell them that the seeds have sprouted, the roots are strong, and I just saw more than five hundred branches that are ready to grow again. Congratulations on your graduation.

AN HONEST GOVERNMENT,
A HOPEFUL FUTURE
A Speech At The University of Nairobi
August 28, 2006

(Nairobi, Kenya) Barack Obama delivered this speech at the University of Nairobi, taking as his theme honesty in government: *Corruption has a way of magnifying the very worst twists of fate. It makes it impossible to respond effectively to crises—whether it's the HIV/AIDS pandemic or malaria or crippling drought. What's worse—corruption can also provide opportunities for those who would harness the fear and hatred of others to their agenda and ambitions.*

The first time I came to Kenya was in 1987. I had just finished three years of work as a community organizer in low-income neighborhoods of Chicago, and was about to enroll in law school. My sister, Auma, was teaching that year at this university, and so I came to stay with her for a month.

My experience then was very different than it has been on this trip. Instead of a motorcade, we traveled in my sister's old VW Beetle, which even then was already ten years old. When it broke down in front of Uhuru Park, we had to push until some joakalis came to fix it by the side of the road. I slept on the couch of my sister's apartment, not a fancy hotel, and often took my meals at a small tea-house in downtown Nairobi. When we went upcountry, we traveled by train and matatu, with chickens and collard greens and sometimes babies placed in my lap.

But it was a magical trip. To begin with, I discovered the warmth and sense of community that the people of Kenya possess—their sense of hopefulness even in the face of great difficulty. I discovered the beauty of the land, a beauty that haunts you long after you've left.

And most importantly for me, I discovered the story of my father's life, and the story of his father before him.

I learned that my grandfather had been a cook for the British and, although he was a respected elder in his village, he was called "boy" by his employers for most of his life. I learned about the brutal repression of Operation Anvil, the days of rape and torture in the Pipeline camps, the lives that so many gave, and how my grandfather had been arrested briefly during this period, despite being at the periphery of Kenya's liberation struggles.

I learned how my father had grown up in a tiny village called Alego, near Siaya, during this period of tumult. I began to understand and appreciate the distance he had traveled—from being a boy herding goats to a student at the University of Hawaii and Harvard University to the respected economist that he was upon his return to Kenya. In many ways, he embodied the new Africa of the early '60s, a man who had obtained the knowledge of the Western world, and sought to bring it back home, where he hoped he could help create a new nation.

And yet, I discovered that for all his education, my father's life ended up being filled with disappointments. His ideas about how Kenya should progress often put him at odds with the politics of tribe and patronage, and because he spoke his mind, sometimes to a fault, he ended up being fired from his job and prevented from finding work in the country for many, many years. And on a more personal level, because he never fully reconciled the traditions of his village with more modern conceptions of family— because he related to women as his father had, expecting them to obey him no matter what he did—his family life was unstable, and his children never knew him well.

In many ways, then, my family's life reflects some of the contradictions of Kenya, and indeed, the African continent as a whole. The history of Africa is a history of ancient kingdoms and great traditions; the story of people fighting to be free from colonial rule; the heroism of not only of great men like Nkrumah and Kenyatta and Mandela, but also ordinary people who endured great hardship—from Ghana to South Africa—to secure self-determination in the face of great odds.

But for all the progress that has been made, we must surely acknowledge that neither Kenya nor the African continent have yet fulfilled their potential—that the hopefulness of the post-colonial era has been replaced by cynicism and sometimes despair, and that true freedom has not yet been won for those struggling to live on less than a few shillings a day, for those who have fallen prey to HIV/AIDS or malaria, to those ordinary citizens who continue to find themselves trapped in the crossfire of war or ethnic conflict.

One statistic powerfully describes this unfulfilled promise. In the early 1960's, as Kenya was gaining its independence, its gross national product was not very different from that of South Korea. Today, South Korea's economy is forty times larger than Kenya's.

How can we explain this fact? Certainly it is not due to lack of effort on the part of ordinary Kenyans. We know how hard Kenyans are willing to work, the tremendous sacrifices that Kenyan mothers make for their children, the Herculean efforts that Kenyan fathers make for their families. We know as well the talent, the intelligence, and the creativity that exists in this country. And we know how much this land is blessed—just as the entire African continent is blessed—with great gifts and riches.

So what explains this? I believe there a number of factors at work.

Kenya, like many African nations, did not come of age under the best historical circumstances. It suffers from the legacy of colonialism, of national boundaries that were drawn without regard to the political and tribal alignments of indigenous peoples, and that therefore fed conflict and tribal strife.

Kenya was also forced to rapidly move from a highly agrarian to a more urban, industrialized nation. This means that the education and health care systems—issues that my own nation more than two hundred years old still struggles with—lag behind, impacting its development.

Third, Kenya is hurt from factors unique to Africa's geography and place in the world— disease, distance from viable markets and especially terms of trade. When African nations were just gaining independence, industrialized nations had decades of experience building their domestic economies and navigating the international financial system. And, as Frederick Douglass once stated:

"Power concedes nothing without a demand. It never did, and it never will."

As a result, many African nations have been asked to liberalize their markets without reciprocal concessions from mature economies. This lack of access for Africa's agriculture and commodities has restricted an important engine of economic growth.

Other issues, such as resource extraction and the drain of human capital have also been major factors.

As a Senator from the United States, I believe that my country, and other nations, have an obligation and self-interest in being full partners with Kenya and with Africa. And I will do my part to shape an intelligent foreign policy that promotes peace and prosperity. A foreign policy that gives hope and opportunity to the people of this great continent.

But Kenya must do its part. It cannot wait for other nations to act first. The hard truth is that nations, by and large, will act in their self-interest and, if Kenya does not act, it will fall behind.

It's more than just history and outside influences that explain why Kenya lags behind. Like many nations across this continent, where Kenya is failing is in its ability to create a government that is transparent and accountable. One that serves its people and is free from corruption.

There is no doubt that what Kenyans have accomplished with this independence is both impressive and inspiring. Among African nations, Kenya remains a model for representative democracy—a place where many different ethnic factions have found a way to live and work together in peace and stability. You enjoy a robust civil society; a press that's free, fair, and honest; and a strong partnership with my own country that has resulted in critical cooperation on terrorist issues, real strides in fighting disease and poverty, and an important alliance on fostering regional stability.

And yet, the reason I speak of the freedom that you fought so hard to win is because today that freedom is in jeopardy. It is being threatened by corruption.

Corruption is not a new problem. It's not just a Kenyan problem, or an African problem. It's a human problem, and it has existed in some form in almost every society. My own city of Chicago has been the home of some of the most corrupt local politics in American history, from patronage machines to questionable elections. In just the last year, our own U.S. Congress has seen a representative resign after taking bribes, and several others fall under investigation for using their public office for private gain.

But while corruption is a problem we all share, here in Kenya it is a crisis—a crisis that's robbing an honest people of the opportunities they have fought for, the opportunity they deserve.

I know that while recent reports have pointed to strong economic growth in this country, fifty-six percent of Kenyans still live in poverty. And I know that the vast majority of people in this country desperately want to change this.

It is painfully obvious that corruption stifles development. It siphons off scarce resources that could improve infrastructure, bolster education systems, and strengthen public health. It stacks the deck so high against entrepreneurs that they cannot get their job-creating ideas off the ground. In fact, one recent survey showed that corruption in Kenya costs local firms six percent of their revenues, the difference between good-paying jobs in Kenya or somewhere else. And corruption also erodes the state from the inside out, sickening the justice system until there is no justice to be found, poisoning the police forces until their presence becomes a source of insecurity rather than comfort.

Corruption has a way of magnifying the very worst twists of fate. It makes it impossible to respond effectively to crises, whether it's the HIV/AIDS pandemic or malaria or crippling drought.

What's worse, corruption can also provide opportunities for those who would harness the fear and hatred of others to their agenda and ambitions.

It can shield a war criminal ... by allowing him to purchase safe haven for a time and robbing all humanity of the opportunity to bring the criminal to justice.

Terrorist attacks—like those that have shed Kenyan blood and struck at the heart of the Kenyan economy—are facilitated by customs and border officers who can be paid off, by police forces so crippled by corruption that they do not protect the personal safety of Kenyans walking the streets of Nairobi, and by forged documents that are easy to find in a climate where graft and fraud thrive.

Some of the worst actors on the international stage can also take advantage of the collective exhaustion and outrage that people feel with official corruption, as we've seen with Islamic extremists who promise purification, but deliver totalitarianism. Endemic corruption opens the door to this kind of movement, and in its wake comes a new set of distortions and betrayals of public trust.

In the end, if the people cannot trust their government to do the job for which it exists—to protect them and to promote their common welfare—all else is lost. And this is why the struggle against corruption is one of the great struggles of our time.

The good news is that there are already signs of progress here. Willingness to report corruption is increasing significantly in Kenya. The Kenyan media has been courageous in uncovering and reporting on some of the most blatant abuses of the system, and there has been a growing recognition among people and politicians that this is a critical issue.

Among other things, this recognition resulted in the coalition that came to power in the December elections of 2002. This coalition succeeded by promising change, and their early gestures ... were all promising.

But elections are not enough. In a true democracy, it is what happens between elections that is the true measure of how a government treats its people.

Today, we're starting to see that the Kenyan people want more than a simple changing of the guard, more than piecemeal reforms to a crisis that's crippling their country. The Kenyan people are crying out for real change, and whether one voted orange or banana in last year's referendum, the message that many Kenyans seemed to be sending was one of dissatisfaction with the pace of reform, and real frustration with continued tolerance of corruption at high levels.

And so we know that there is more work to be done, more reforms to be made. I don't have all the solutions or think that they'll be easy, but there are a few places that a country truly committed to reform could start.

We know that the temptation to take a bribe is greater when you're not making enough on the job. And we also know that the more people there are on the government payroll, the more likely it is that someone will be encouraged to take a bribe. So if the government found ways to downsize the bureaucracy—to cut out the positions that aren't necessary or useful—it could use the extra money to increase the salary of other government officials.

Of course, the best way to reduce bureaucracy and increase pay is to create more private sector jobs. And the way to create good jobs is when the rules of a society are transparent—when there's a clear and advertised set of laws and regulations regarding how to start a business, what it takes to own property, how to go about getting a loan—there is less of a chance that some corrupt bureaucrat will make up his own rules that suit only his interests. Clarifying these rules and focusing resources on building a judicial system that can enforce them and resolve disputes should be a primary goal of any government suffering from corruption.

In addition, we know that the more information the public is provided, the easier it will be for your Kenyan brothers and sisters out in the villages to evaluate whether they are being treated fairly by their public servants or not. Wealth declarations do little good if no one can access them, and accountability in government spending is not possible if no one knows how much was available and allocated to a given project in the first place.

Finally, ethnic-based tribal politics has to stop. It is rooted in the bankrupt idea that the goal of politics or business is to funnel as much of the pie as possible to one's family, tribe, or circle with little regard for the public good. It stifles innovation and fractures the fabric of the society. Instead of opening businesses and engaging in commerce, people come to rely on patronage and payback as a means of advancing. Instead of unifying the country to move forward on solving problems, it divides neighbor from neighbor.

An accountable, transparent government can break this cycle. When people are judged by merit, not connections, then the best and brightest can lead the country, people will work hard, and the entire economy will grow. Everyone will benefit and more resources will be available for all, not just select groups.

Of course, in the end, one of the strongest weapons your country has against corruption is the ability of you, the people, to stand up and speak out about the injustices you see. The Kenyan people are the ultimate guardians against abuses.

The world knows the names of Wangari Maathai and John Githongo, who are fighting against the insidious corruption that has weakened Kenya. But there are so many others, some of whom I'm meeting during my visit here.... As well as numerous

Kenyan men and women who have refused to pay bribes to get civil servants to perform their duties; the auditors and inspectors general who have done the job before them accurately and fairly, regardless of where the facts have led; the journalists who asked questions and pushed for answers when it may have been more lucrative to look the other way, or whip up a convenient fiction. And then there are anonymous Kenyan whistleblowers who show us what is, so that we can all work together to demand what should be.

By rejecting the insulting idea that corruption is somehow a part of Kenyan culture, these heroes reveal the very opposite—they reveal a strength and integrity of character that can build a great country, a great future. By focusing on building strong, independent institutions, like an anti-corruption commission with real authority, rather than cults of personality, they make a contribution to their country that will last longer than their own lives. They fight the fight of our time.

Looking out at this crowd of young people, I have faith that you will fight this fight too.

You will decide if your leaders will be held accountable, or if you will look the other way.

You will decide if the standards and the rules will be the same for everyone, regardless of ethnicity or of wealth.

And you will determine the direction of this country in the 21st Century—whether the hard work of the many is lost to the selfish desires of a few, or whether you build an open, honest, stronger Kenya where everyone rises together.

This is the Kenya that so many who came before you envisioned—all those men and women who struggled and sacrificed and fought for the freedom you enjoy today.

I know that honoring their memory and making that freedom real may seem like an impossible task—an effort bigger than you can imagine—but sometimes all it takes to move us there is doing what little you can to right the wrongs you see.

As I said at the outset, I did not know my father well. He returned to Kenya from America when I was still young. Since that time I have known him through stories—those my mother would tell and those I heard from my relatives here in Kenya on my last trip to this country.

I know from these stories that my father was not a perfect man, that he made his share of mistakes and disappointed his share of people in his lifetime.

As our parents' children, we have the opportunity to learn from these mistakes and disappointments. We have the opportunity to muster the courage to fulfill the promise of our forefathers and lead our great nations towards a better future.

In today's Kenya—a Kenya already more open and less repressive than in my father's day—it is that courage that will bring the reform so many of you so desperately want and deserve. I wish all of you luck in finding this courage in the days and months to come, and I want you to know that as your ally, your friend, and your brother, I will be there to help in any way I can.

THE LEGACY OF
DR. MARTIN LUTHER KING, JR.
A Speech At The Martin Luther King Memorial
November 13, 2006

(Washington, D.C.) Barack Obama delivered this speech on the life and legacy of Dr. Martin Luther King, Jr. at the ground-breaking ceremony for a Memorial to the slain civil rights leader on the National Mall: *Like Moses before him, he would never live to see the Promised Land. But from the mountain top, he pointed the way for us.*

I have two daughters, ages five and eight. And when I see the plans for this memorial, I think about what it will be like when I first bring them here upon the memorial's completion. I imagine us walking down to this tidal basin, between one memorial dedicated to the man who helped give birth to a nation, and another dedicated to the man who preserved it. I picture us walking beneath the shadows cast by the Mountain of Despair, and gazing up at the Stone of Hope, and reading the quotes on the wall together as the water falls like rain.

And at some point, I know that one of my daughters, perhaps my youngest, will ask,

"Daddy, why is this monument here? What did this man do?"

How might I answer them? Unlike the others commemorated in this place, Dr. Martin Luther King Jr. was not a president of the United States—at no time in his life did he hold public office. He was not a hero of foreign wars. He never had much money, and while he lived he was reviled at least as much as he was celebrated. By his own accounts, he was a man frequently racked with doubt, a man not without flaws, a man who, like Moses before him, more than once questioned why he had been chosen for so arduous a task—the task of leading a people to freedom, the task of healing the festering wounds of a nation's original sin.

And yet lead a nation he did. Through words he gave voice to the voiceless. Through deeds he gave courage to the faint of heart. By dint of vision, and determination, and most of all faith in the redeeming power of love, he endured the humiliation of arrest, the loneliness of a prison cell, the constant threats to his life, until he finally inspired a nation to transform itself, and begin to live up to the meaning of its creed.

Like Moses before him, he would never live to see the Promised Land. But from the mountain top, he pointed the way for us—a land no longer torn asunder with racial hatred and ethnic strife, a land that measured itself by how it treats the least of these, a land in which strength is defined not simply by the capacity to wage war but by the determination to forge peace—a land in which all of God's children might come together in a spirit of brotherhood.

We have not yet arrived at this longed for place. For all the progress we have made, there are times when the land of our dreams recedes from us—when we are lost, wandering spirits, content with our suspicions and our angers, our long-held grudges and petty disputes, our frantic diversions and tribal allegiances.

And yet, by erecting this monument, we are reminded that this different, better place beckons us, and that we will find it not across distant hills or within some hidden valley, but rather we will find it somewhere in our hearts.

In the Book of Micah, Chapter 6, verse 8, the prophet says that God has already told us what is good.

"What doth the Lord require of thee," the verse tells us, "but to do justly, and to love mercy, and to walk humbly with thy God?"

The man we honor today did what God required. In the end, that is what I will tell my daughters—I will leave it to their teachers and their history books to tell them the rest. As Dr. King asked to be remembered, I will tell them that this man gave his life serving others. I will tell them that this man tried to love somebody. I will tell them that because he did these things, they live today with the freedom God intended, their citizenship unquestioned, their dreams unbounded. And I will tell them that they too can love. That they too can serve. And that each generation is beckoned anew—to fight for what is right, and strive for what is just, and to find within itself the spirit, the sense of purpose, that can remake a nation and transform a world.

WITHDRAWAL FROM IRAQ
A Speech To The
Chicago Council on Global Affairs
November 20, 2006

(Chicago, Illinois) Barack Obama delivered this speech to the Chicago Council on Global Affairs, taking as his theme the ongoing War in Iraq: *The time for waiting in Iraq is over. It is time to change our policy. It is time to give Iraqis their country back. And it is time to refocus America's efforts on the wider struggle yet to be won.*

Throughout American history, there have been moments that call on us to meet the challenges of an uncertain world, and pay whatever price is required to secure our freedom.

They are the soul-trying times our forbearers spoke of, when the ease of complacency and self-interest must give way to the more difficult task of rendering judgment on what is best for the nation and for posterity, and then acting on that judgment—making the hard choices and sacrifices necessary to uphold our most deeply held values and ideals.

This was true for those who went to Lexington and Concord. It was true for those who lie buried at Gettysburg. It was true for those who built democracy's arsenal to vanquish fascism, and who then built a series of alliances and a world order that would ultimately defeat communism.

And this has been true for those of us who looked on the rubble and ashes of 9/11, and made a solemn pledge that such an atrocity would never again happen on United States soil, that we would do whatever it took to hunt down those responsible, and use every tool at our disposal—diplomatic, economic, and military—to root out both the agents of terrorism and the conditions that helped breed it.

In each case, what has been required to meet the challenges we face has been good judgment and clear vision from our leaders, and a fundamental seriousness and engagement on the part of the American people—a willingness on the part of each of us to look past what is petty and small and sensational, and look ahead to what is necessary and purposeful.

A few Tuesdays ago, the American people embraced this serious-ness with regards to America's policy in Iraq. Americans were originally persuaded by the President to go to war in part because of the threat of weapons of mass destruction, and in part because they were told that it would help reduce the threat of international terrorism.

Neither turned out to be true. And now, after three long years of watching the same back and forth in Washington, the American people have sent a clear message that the days of using the war on terror as a political football are over. That policy-by-slogan will no longer pass as an acceptable form of debate in this country. "Mission accomplished," "cut and run," "stay the course"— the American people have determined that all these phrases have become meaningless in the face of a conflict that grows more deadly and chaotic with each passing day, a conflict that has only increased the terrorist threat it was supposed to help contain.

2,867 Americans have now died in this war. Thousands more have suffered wounds that will last a lifetime. Iraq is descending into chaos based on ethnic divisions that were around long before American troops arrived. The conflict has left us distracted from containing the world's growing threats—in North Korea, in Iran, and in Afghanistan. And a report by our own intelligence agencies has concluded that al Qaeda is successfully using the war in Iraq to recruit a new generation of terrorists for its war on America.

These are serious times for our country, and with their votes two weeks ago, Americans demanded a feasible strategy with defined goals in Iraq—a strategy no longer driven by ideology and politics, but one that is based on a realistic assessment of the sobering facts on the ground and our interests in the region.

This kind of realism has been missing since the very conception of this war, and it is what led me to publicly oppose it in 2002. The notion that Iraq would quickly and easily become a bulwark of flourishing democracy in the Middle East was not a plan for victory, but an ideological fantasy. I said then and believe now that Saddam Hussein was a ruthless dictator who craved weapons of mass destruction but posed no imminent threat to the United States; that a war in Iraq would harm, not help, our efforts to defeat al Qaeda and finish the job in Afghanistan; and that an invasion would require an occupation of undetermined length, at undetermined cost, with undetermined consequences.

Month after month, and then year after year, I've watched with a heavy heart as my deepest suspicions about this war's conception have been confirmed and exacerbated in its disastrous implementation. No matter how bad it gets, we are told to wait, and not ask questions. We have been assured that the insurgency is in its last throes. We have been told that progress is just around the corner, and that when the Iraqis stand up, we will be able to stand down. Last week, without a trace of irony, the President even chose Vietnam as the backdrop for remarks counseling "patience" with his policies in Iraq.

When I came here and gave a speech on this war a year ago, I suggested that we begin to move towards a phased redeployment of American troops from Iraqi soil. At that point, seventy-five U.S. Senators, Republican and Democrat, including myself, had also voted in favor of a resolution demanding that 2006 be a year of significant transition in Iraq.

What we have seen instead is a year of significant deterioration. A year in which well-respected Republicans like John Warner, former Administration officials like Colin Powell, generals who have served in Iraq, and intelligence experts have all said that what we are doing is not working. A year that is ending with an attempt by the bipartisan Iraq Study Group to determine what can be done about a country that is quickly spiraling out of control.

According to our own Pentagon, the situation on the ground is now pointing towards chaos. Sectarian violence has reached an all-time high, and 365,000 Iraqis have fled their homes since the bombing of a Shia mosque in Samarra last February. 300,000 Iraqi security forces have supposedly been recruited and trained over the last two years, and yet American troop levels have not been reduced by a single soldier. The addition of 4,000 American troops in Baghdad has not succeeded in securing that increasingly perilous city. And polls show that almost two-thirds of all Iraqis now sympathize with attacks on American soldiers.

Prime Minister Maliki is not making our job easier. In just the past three weeks, he has—and I'm quoting from a *New York Times* article here—"rejected the notion of an American 'timeline' for action on urgent Iraqi political issues; ordered American commanders to lift checkpoints they had set up around the Shiite district of Sadr City to hunt for a kidnapped American soldier and a fugitive Shiite death squad leader; and blamed the Americans for the deteriorating security situation in Iraq."

This is now the reality of Iraq.

Now, I am hopeful that the Iraq Study Group emerges next month with a series of proposals around which we can begin to build a bipartisan consensus. I am committed to working with this White House and any of my colleagues in the months to come to craft such a consensus. And I believe that it remains possible to salvage an acceptable outcome to this long and misguided war.

But it will not be easy. For the fact is that there are no good options left in this war. There are no options that do not carry significant risks. And so the question is not whether there is some magic formula for success, or guarantee against failure, in Iraq. Rather, the question is what strategies, imperfect though they may be, are most likely to achieve the best outcome in Iraq, one that will ultimately put us on a more effective course to deal with international terrorism, nuclear proliferation, and other critical threats to our security.

What is absolutely clear is that it is not enough for the President to respond to Iraq's reality by saying that he is "open to" or "interested in" new ideas while acting as if all that's required is doing more of the same. It is not enough for him to simply lay out benchmarks for progress with no consequences attached for failing to meet them. And it is not enough for the President to tell us that victory in this war is simply a matter of American resolve. The American people have been extraordinarily resolved. They have seen their sons and daughters killed or wounded in the streets of Fallujah. They have spent hundreds of billions of their hard-earned dollars on this effort—money that could have been devoted to strengthening our homeland security and our competitive standing as a nation. No, it has not been a failure of resolve that has led us to this chaos, but a failure of strategy—and that strategy must change.

It may be politically advantageous for the President to simply define victory as staying and defeat as leaving, but it prevents a serious conversation about the realistic objectives we can still achieve in Iraq. Dreams of democracy and hopes for a perfect government are now just that—dreams and hopes. We must instead turn our focus to those concrete objectives that are possible to attain, namely, preventing Iraq from becoming what Afghanistan once was, maintaining our influence in the Middle East, and forging a political settlement to stop the sectarian violence so that our troops can come home.

There is no reason to believe that more of the same will achieve these objectives in Iraq. And, while some have proposed escalating this war by adding thousands of more troops, there is little reason to believe that this will achieve these results either. It's not clear that these troop levels are sustainable for a significant period of time, and, according to our commanders on the ground, adding American forces will only relieve the Iraqis from doing more on their own. Moreover, without a coherent strategy or better cooperation from the Iraqis, we would only be putting more of our soldiers in the crossfire of a civil war.

Let me underscore this point. The American soldiers I met when I traveled to Iraq this year were performing their duties with bravery, with brilliance, and without question. They are doing so today. They have battled insurgents, secured cities, and maintained some semblance of order in Iraq. But even as they have carried out their responsibilities with excellence and valor, they have also told me that there is no military solution to this war. Our troops can help suppress the violence, but they cannot solve its root causes. And all the troops in the world won't be able to force Shia, Sunni, and Kurd to sit down at a table, resolve their differences, and forge a lasting peace.

I have long said that the only solution in Iraq is a political one. To reach such a solution, we must communicate clearly and effectively to the factions in Iraq that the days of asking, urging, and waiting for them to take control of their own country are coming to an end. No more coddling, no more equivocation. Our best hope for success is to use the tools we have—military, financial, diplomatic—to pressure the Iraqi leadership to finally come to a political agreement between the warring factions that can create some sense of stability in the country and bring this conflict under control.

The first part of this strategy begins by exerting the greatest leverage we have on the Iraqi government—a phased redeployment of U.S. troops from Iraq on a timetable that would begin in four to six months.

When I first advocated steps along these lines over a year ago, I had hoped that this phased redeployment could begin by the end of 2006. Such a timetable may now need to begin in 2007, but begin it must. For only through this phased redeployment can we send a clear message to the Iraqi factions that the U.S. is not going to hold together this country indefinitely, that it will be up to them to form a viable government that can effectively run and secure Iraq.

Let me be more specific. The President should announce to the Iraqi people that our policy will include a gradual and substantial reduction in U.S. forces. He should then work with our military commanders to map out the best plan for such a redeployment and determine precise levels and dates. When possible, this should be done in consultation with the Iraqi government, but it should not depend on Iraqi approval.

I am not suggesting that this timetable be overly rigid. We cannot compromise the safety of our troops, and we should be willing to adjust to realities on the ground. The redeployment could be temporarily suspended if the parties in Iraq reach an effective political arrangement that stabilizes the situation and they offer us a clear and compelling rationale for maintaining certain troop levels. Moreover, it could be suspended if at any point U.S. commanders believe that a further reduction would put American troops in danger.

Drawing down our troops in Iraq will allow us to redeploy additional troops to Northern Iraq and elsewhere in the in the region as an over-the-horizon force. This force could help prevent the conflict in Iraq from becoming a wider war, consolidate gains in Northern Iraq, reassure allies in the Gulf, allow our troops to strike directly at al Qaeda wherever it may exist, and demonstrate to international terrorist organizations that they have not driven us from the region.

Perhaps most importantly, some of these troops could be redeployed to Afghanistan, where our lack of focus and commitment of resources has led to an increasing deterioration of the security situation there. The President's decision to go to war in Iraq has had disastrous consequences for Afghanistan—we have seen a fierce Taliban offensive, a spike in terrorist attacks, and a narco-trafficking problem spiral out of control. Instead of consolidating the gains made by the Karzai government, we are backsliding towards chaos. By redeploying from Iraq to Afghanistan, we will answer NATO's call for more troops and provide a much-needed boost to this critical fight against terrorism.

As a phased redeployment is executed, the majority of the U.S. troops remaining in Iraq should be dedicated to the critical but less visible roles of protecting logistics supply points, critical infrastructure, and American enclaves like the Green Zone, as well as acting as a rapid reaction force to respond to emergencies and go after terrorists.

In such a scenario, it is conceivable that a significantly reduced U.S. force might remain in Iraq for a more extended period of time. But only if U.S. commanders think such a force would be effective; if there is substantial movement towards a political solution among Iraqi factions; if the Iraqi government showed a serious commitment to disbanding the militias; and if the Iraqi government asked us—in a public and unambiguous way—for such continued support. We would make clear in such a scenario that the United States would not be maintaining permanent military bases in Iraq, but would do what was necessary to help prevent a total collapse of the Iraqi state and further polarization of Iraqi society. Such a reduced but active presence will also send a clear message to hostile countries like Iran and Syria that we intend to remain a key player in this region.

The second part of our strategy should be to couple this phased redeployment with a more effective plan that puts the Iraqi security forces in the lead, intensifies and focuses our efforts to train those forces, and expands the numbers of our personnel—especially special forces—who are deployed with Iraqi units advisers.

An increase in the quality and quantity of U.S. personnel in training and advisory roles can guard against militia infiltration of Iraqi units; develop the trust and goodwill of Iraqi soldiers and the local populace; and lead to better intelligence while undercutting grassroots support for the insurgents.

Let me emphasize one vital point—any U.S. strategy must address the problem of sectarian militias in Iraq. In the absence of a genuine commitment on the part of all of the factions in Iraq to deal with this issue, it is doubtful that a unified Iraqi government can function for long, and it is doubtful that U.S. forces, no matter how large, can prevent an escalation of widespread sectarian killing.

Of course, in order to convince the various factions to embark on the admittedly difficult task of disarming their militias, the Iraqi government must also make headway on reforming the institutions that support the military and the police. We can teach the soldiers to fight and police to patrol, but if the Iraqi government will not properly feed, adequately pay, or provide them with the equipment they need, they will continue to desert in large numbers, or maintain fealty only to their religious group rather than the national government. The security forces have to be far more inclusive. Standing up an army composed mainly of Shiites and Kurds will only cause the Sunnis to feel more threatened and fight even harder.

The third part of our strategy should be to link continued economic aid in Iraq with the existence of tangible progress toward a political settlement.

So far, Congress has given the Administration unprecedented flexibility in determining how to spend more than $20 billion dollars in Iraq. But instead of effectively targeting this aid, we have seen some of the largest waste, fraud, and abuse of foreign aid in American history. Today, the Iraqi landscape is littered with ill-conceived, half-finished projects that have done almost nothing to help the Iraqi people or stabilize the country.

This must end in the next session of Congress, when we reassert our authority to oversee the management of this war. This means no more bloated no-bid contracts that cost the taxpayers millions in overhead and administrative expenses.

We need to continue to provide some basic reconstruction funding that will be used to put Iraqis to work and help our troops stabilize key areas. But we need to also move towards more condition-based aid packages where economic assistance is contingent upon the ability of Iraqis to make measurable progress on reducing sectarian violence and forging a lasting political settlement.

Finally, we have to realize that the entire Middle East has an enormous stake in the outcome of Iraq, and we must engage neighboring countries in finding a solution.

This includes opening dialogue with both Syria and Iran, an idea supported by both James Baker and Robert Gates. We know these countries want us to fail, and we should remain steadfast in our opposition to their support of terrorism and Iran's nuclear ambitions. But neither Iran nor Syria want to see a security vacuum in Iraq filled with chaos, terrorism, refugees, and violence, as it could have a destabilizing effect throughout the entire region, and within their own countries.

And so I firmly believe that we should convene a regional conference with the Iraqis, Saudis, Iranians, Syrians, the Turks, Jordanians, the British and others. The goal of this conference should be to get foreign fighters out of Iraq, prevent a further descent into civil war, and push the various Iraqi factions towards a political solution.

Make no mistake—if the Iranians and Syrians think they can use Iraq as another Afghanistan or a staging area from which to attack Israel or other countries, they are badly mistaken. It is in our national interest to prevent this from happening. We should also make it clear that, even after we begin to draw down forces, we will still work with our allies in the region to combat international terrorism and prevent the spread of weapons of mass destruction. It is simply not productive for us not to engage in discussions with Iran and Syria on an issue of such fundamental importance to all of us.

This brings me to a set of broader points. As we change strategy in Iraq, we should also think about what Iraq has taught us about America's strategy in the wider struggle against rogue threats and international terrorism.

Many who supported the original decision to go to war in Iraq have argued that it has been a failure of implementation. But I have long believed it has also been a failure of conception, that the rationale behind the war itself was misguided. And so, going forward, I believe there are strategic lessons to be learned from this as we continue to confront the new threats of this new century.

The first is that we should be more modest in our belief that we can impose democracy on a country through military force. In the past, it has been movements for freedom from within tyrannical regimes that have led to flourishing democracies, movements that continue today. This doesn't mean abandoning our values and ideals; wherever we can, it's in our interest to help foster democracy through the diplomatic and economic resources at our disposal. But even as we provide such help, we should be clear that the institutions of democracy—free markets, a free press, a strong civil society—cannot be built overnight, and they cannot be built at the end of a barrel of a gun. And so we must realize that the freedoms FDR once spoke of—especially freedom from want and freedom from fear—do not just come from deposing a tyrant and handing out ballots; they are only realized once the personal and material security of a people is ensured as well.

The second lesson is that in any conflict, it is not enough to simply plan for war; you must also plan for success. Much has been written about how the military invasion of Iraq was planned without any thought to what political situation we would find after Baghdad fell. Such lack of foresight is simply inexcusable. If we commit our troops anywhere in the world, it is our solemn responsibility to define their mission and formulate a viable plan to fulfill that mission and bring our troops home.

The final lesson is that in an interconnected world, the defeat of international terrorism—and most importantly, the prevention of these terrorist organizations from obtaining weapons of mass destruction—will require the cooperation of many nations. We must always reserve the right to strike unilaterally at terrorists wherever they may exist. But we should know that our success in doing so is enhanced by engaging our allies so that we receive the crucial diplomatic, military, intelligence, and financial support that can lighten our load and add legitimacy to our actions. This means talking to our friends and, at times, even our enemies.

We need to keep these lessons in mind as we think about the broader threats America now faces—threats we haven't paid nearly enough attention to because we have been distracted in Iraq.

The National Intelligence Estimate, which details how we're creating more terrorists in Iraq than we're defeating, is the most obvious example of how the war is hurting our efforts in the larger battle against terrorism. But there are many others.

The overwhelming presence of our troops, our intelligence, and our resources in Iraq has stretched our military to the breaking point and distracted us from the growing threats of a dangerous world. The Chairman of the Joint Chiefs recently said that if a conflict arose in North Korea, we'd have to largely rely on the Navy and Air Force to take care of it, since the Army and Marines are engaged elsewhere. In my travels to Africa, I have seen weak governments and broken societies that can be exploited by al Qaeda. And on a trip to the former Soviet Union, I have seen the biological and nuclear weapons terrorists could easily steal while the world looks the other way.

There is one other place where our mistakes in Iraq have cost us dearly—and that is the loss of our government's credibility with the American people. According to a Pew survey, forty-two percent of Americans now agree with the statement that the U.S. should "mind its own business internationally and let other countries get along the best they can on their own."

We cannot afford to be a country of isolationists right now. 9/11 showed us that, try as we might to ignore the rest of the world, our enemies will no longer ignore us. And so we need to maintain a strong foreign policy, relentless in pursuing our enemies and hopeful in promoting our values around the world. But to guard against isolationist sentiments in this country, we must change conditions in Iraq and the policy that has characterized our time there—a policy based on blind hope and ideology instead of fact and reality.

Americans called for this more serious policy a few Tuesdays ago. It's time that we listen to their concerns and win back their trust. I spoke here a year ago and delivered a message about Iraq that was similar to the one I did today. I refuse to accept the possibility that I will have to come back a year from now and say the same thing.

There have been too many speeches. There have been too many excuses. There have been too many flag-draped coffins, and there have been too many heartbroken families.

The time for waiting in Iraq is over. It is time to change our policy. It is time to give Iraqis their country back. And it is time to refocus America's efforts on the wider struggle yet to be won.

WE ARE ALL SICK BECAUSE OF AIDS
The World AIDS Day Speech
December 1, 2006

(Orange County, California) Barack Obama delivered this speech at "The Race Against Time," the 2006 Global Summit on AIDS and the Church, taking as his theme the moral imperative of the fight against HIV and AIDS: *We are all sick because of AIDS—and we are all tested by this crisis.*

I took my own trip to Africa a few months ago.... [I]t's an experience that stays with you for quite some time. I visited an HIV/AIDS hospital in South Africa that was filled to capacity with people who walked hours, even days, just for the chance to seek help. I met courageous patients who refused to give up for themselves or their families. And I came across AIDS activists who meet resistance from their own government but keep on fighting anyway.

But of all that I heard, I encountered few stories as heartbreaking as the one recently told by Laurie Goering, a *Chicago Tribune* reporter based in Johannesburg who had covered our trip for her newspaper.

Three years ago, Laurie hired a woman named Hlengiwe Leocardia Mchunu as her nanny. Leo, as she is known, grew up as one of nine children in a small South African village. All through her life, she worked hard to raise her two kids and save every last penny she earned, and by the time Leo was hired as Laurie's nanny, she had almost finished paying off the mortgage on her home. She had even hoped to use the extra money from her new job to open a refuge for local children who had been orphaned by AIDS.

Then one day, Leo received a phone call that her eldest brother had fallen ill. At first he told everyone it was diabetes, but later, in the hospital, admitted to the family it was AIDS. He died a few days later. His wife succumbed to the disease as well. And Leo took in their three children.

Six months later, Leo got another phone call. Her younger brother had also become sick with AIDS. She cared for him and nursed him as she did her first brother, but he soon died as well.

Leo's pregnant sister was next. And then another brother. And then another brother.

She paid for their caskets and their funerals. She took in their children and paid for their schooling. She ran out of money, and she borrowed what she could. She ran out again, and she borrowed even more.

And still, the phone calls continued. All across her tiny village, Leo watched more siblings and cousins and nieces and nephews test positive for HIV. She saw neighbors lose their families. She saw a grandmother house sixteen orphaned grandchildren under her roof. And she saw some children go hungry because there was no one to care for them at all.

You know, AIDS is a story often told by numbers. Forty million infected with HIV. Nearly 4.5 million this year alone. Twelve million orphans in Africa. Eight thousand deaths and six thousand new infections every single day. In some places, ninety percent of those with HIV do not know they have it. And we just learned that AIDS is set to become the third leading cause of death worldwide in the coming years.

They are staggering, these numbers, and they help us understand the magnitude of this pandemic. But when repeated by themselves, statistics can also numb—they can hide the individual stories and tragedies and hopes of the Leos who live the daily drama of this disease.

On this World AIDS day, these are the stories that the world needs to hear. They are the stories that touch our souls—and that call us to action.

I cannot begin to imagine what it would be like if Leo's family was my own. If I had to answer those phone calls, if I had to attend those funerals. All I know is that no matter how or why my family became sick, I would be called to care for them and comfort them and do what I could to help find a cure. I know every one of you would do the same if it were your family.

Here's the thing—my faith tells me that Leo's family is my family.

We are all sick because of AIDS, and we are all tested by this crisis. It is a test not only of our willingness to respond, but of our ability to look past the artificial divisions and debates that have often shaped that response. When you go to places like Africa and you see this problem up close, you realize that it's not a question of either treatment or prevention, or even what kind of prevention. It is all of the above. It is not an issue of either science or values. It is both. Yes, there must be more money spent on this disease. But there must also be a change in hearts and minds, in cultures and attitudes. Neither philanthropist nor scientist, neither government nor church, can solve this problem on their own—AIDS must be an all-hands-on-deck effort.

Let's talk about what these efforts involve. First, if we hope to win this fight, we must stop new infections. We must do what we can to prevent people from contracting HIV in the first place.

Now, too often, the issue of prevention has been framed in "either/or" terms. For some, the only way to prevent the disease is for men and women to change their sexual behavior—in particular, to abstain from sexual activity outside of marriage. For others, such a prescription is unrealistic; they argue that we need to provide people with the tools they need to protect themselves from the virus, regardless of their sexual practices—in particular, by increasing the use of condoms, as well as by developing new methods, like microbicides, that women can initiate themselves to prevent transmission during sex. And in the debate surrounding how we should tackle the scourge of AIDS, we often see each side questioning the other's motives, and thereby impeding progress.

For me, this is a false argument. Let me say this—I don't think we can deny that there is a moral and spiritual component to prevention—that in too many places all over the world where AIDS is prevalent, including our own country, by the way, the relationship between men and women, between sexuality and spirituality, has broken down, and needs to be repaired.

It was striking to see this as I traveled through South Africa and Kenya. Again and again, I heard stories of men and women contracting HIV because sex was no longer part of a sacred covenant, but a mechanical physical act; because men had visited prostitutes and brought the disease home to their wives, or young girls had been subjected to rape and abuse.

These are issues of prevention we cannot walk away from. When a husband thinks it's acceptable to hide his infidelity from his wife, it's not only a sin, it's a potential death sentence. And when rape is still seen as a woman's fault and a woman's shame, but promiscuity is a man's prerogative, it is a problem of the heart that no government can solve. It is, however, a place where local ministries and churches … can, and have, made a real difference—by providing people with a moral framework to make better choices.

Having said that, I also believe that we cannot ignore that abstinence and fidelity may too often be the ideal and not the reality—that we are dealing with flesh and blood men and women and not abstractions—and that if condoms and potentially microbicides can prevent millions of deaths, they should be made more widely available. I know that there are those who, out of sincere religious conviction, oppose such measures. And with these folks, I must respectfully but unequivocally disagree. I do not accept the notion that those who make mistakes in their lives should be given an effective death sentence. Nor am I willing to stand by and allow those who are entirely innocent—wives who, because of the culture they live in, often have no power to refuse sex with their husbands, or children who are born with the infection as a consequence of their parent's behavior—suffer when condoms or other measures would have kept them from harm.

Another area where we can make significant progress in prevention is by removing the stigma that goes along with getting tested for HIV/AIDS. The idea that in some places, nine in ten people with HIV have no idea they're infected is more than frightening—it's a ticking time bomb waiting to go off.

So we need to show people that, just as there is no shame in going to the doctor for a blood test or a CAT scan or a mammogram, there is no shame in going for an HIV test. Because while there was once a time when a positive result gave little hope, today the earlier you know, the faster you can get help. My wife Michelle and I were able to take the test on our trip to Africa, after the Center for Disease Control informed us that by getting a simple fifteen minute test, we may have encouraged as many as half-a-million Kenyans to get tested as well.… I encourage others in public life to do the same. We've got to spread the word to as many people as possible. It's time for us to set an example for others to follow.

Of course, even as we work diligently to slow the rate of new infection, we also have a responsibility to treat the forty million people who are already living with HIV.

In some ways, this should be the easy part. Because we know what works. We know how to save people's lives. We know the medicine is out there and we know that wealthy countries can afford to do more.

That's why it was so frustrating for me to go to South Africa, and see the pain, and see the suffering, and then hear that the country's Minister of Health had promoted the use of beet root, sweet potato, and lemon juice as the best way to cure HIV. Thankfully, the South African government eventually repudiated this, but it's impossible to overestimate how important it is for political leaders like this to set a good example for their people.

We should never forget that God granted us the power to reason so that we would do His work here on Earth—so that we would use science to cure disease, and heal the sick, and save lives. And one of the miracles to come out of the AIDS pandemic is that scientists have discovered medicine that can give people with HIV a new chance at life.

We are called to give them that chance. We have made progress. In South Africa, treatment provided to pregnant women has drastically reduced the incidence of infants born with the infection. But, despite such progress, only one in every five people with HIV around the world is receiving antiretroviral drug treatment. One in every five. We must do better. We should work with drug companies to reduce the costs of generic anti-retroviral drugs, and work with developing nations to help them build the health infrastructure that's necessary to get sick people treated. This means more money for hospitals and medical equipment, and more training for nurses and doctors.

We need a renewed emphasis on nutrition. Right now we're finding out that there are people who are on the drugs, who are getting treatment, who are still dying because they don't have any food to eat. This is inexcusable, especially in countries that have sufficient food supplies. So we must help get them that nutrition, and this is another place where religious organizations that have always provided food to the hungry can help a great deal.

And even as we focus on the enormous crisis in Africa, we need to remember that the problem is not in Africa alone. In the last few years, we have seen an alarming rise in infection rates in the Middle East, Southeast Asia, the former Soviet Union, Eastern Europe, and the Caribbean. And on this World AIDS Day, we cannot forget the crisis occurring in our own backyard. Right here in the United States, AIDS is now the leading cause of death for African-American women aged 25-34, and we are also seeing many poorer and rural communities fail to get the resources they need to deal with their vulnerable populations—a problem that unfortunately some in Congress are trying to address by taking money away from larger cities that are still facing enormous problems of their own.

Now let me say this—I think that President Bush and this past Congress should be applauded for the resources they have contributed to the fight against HIV and AIDS. Through our country's emergency plan for AIDS relief, the United States will have contributed more than $15 billion over five years to combat HIV/AIDS overseas. And the Global Fund, with money from the United States and other countries, has done some heroic work to fight this disease. As I traveled throughout Africa this summer, I was proud of the tangible impact that all this money was having, often through coordinated efforts with the Centers for Disease Control, the State Department, foreign governments, and non-governmental organizations.

So our first priority in Congress should be to reauthorize this program when it expires in 2008. Our second priority should be to reassess what's worked and what hasn't so that we're not wasting one dollar that could be saving someone's life.

But our third priority should be to actually boost our contribution to this effort. With all that is left to be done in this struggle—with all the other areas of the world that need our help—it's time for us to add at least an additional $1 billion a year in new money over the next five years to strengthen and expand the program to places like Southeast Asia, India, and Eastern Europe, where the pandemic will soon reach crisis proportions.

Of course, given all the strains that have been placed on the U.S. budget, and given the extraordinary needs that we face here at home, it may be hard to find the money. But I believe we must try. I believe it will prove to be a wise investment. The list of reasons for us to care about AIDS is long. In an interconnected, globalized world, the ability of pandemics to spread to other countries and continents has never been easier or faster than it is today. There are also security implications, as countries whose populations and economies have been ravaged by AIDS become fertile breeding grounds for civil strife and even terror.

But the reason for us to step up our efforts can't simply be instrumental. There are more fundamental reasons to care. Reasons related to our own humanity. Reasons of the soul.

Like no other illness, AIDS tests our ability to put ourselves in someone else's shoes, to empathize with the plight of our fellow man. While most would agree that the AIDS orphan or the transfusion victim or the wronged wife contracted the disease through no fault of their own, it has too often been easy for some to point to the unfaithful husband or the promiscuous youth or the gay man and say,

"This is your fault. You have sinned."

I don't think that's a satisfactory response. My faith reminds me that we all are sinners.

My faith also tells me that ... it is not a sin to be sick. My Bible tells me that when God sent his only Son to Earth, it was to heal the sick and comfort the weary; to feed the hungry and clothe the naked; to befriend the outcast and redeem those who strayed from righteousness.

Living His example is the hardest kind of faith—but it is surely the most rewarding. It is a way of life that can not only light our way as people of faith, but guide us to a new and better politics as Americans.

For in the end, we must realize that the AIDS orphan in Africa presents us with the same challenge as the gang member in South Central, or the Katrina victim in New Orleans, or the uninsured mother in North Dakota.

We can turn away from these Americans, and blame their problems on themselves, and embrace a politics that's punitive and petty, divisive and small.

Or we can embrace another tradition of politics—a tradition that has stretched from the days of our founding to the glory of the civil rights movement, a tradition based on the simple idea that we have a stake in one another—and that what binds us together is greater than what drives us apart, and that if enough people believe in the truth of that proposition and act on it, then we might not solve every problem, but we can get something meaningful done for the people with whom we share this Earth.

Let me close by returning to the story of Leo, that South African woman burdened by so much death and despair. Sometime after the death of her fifth sibling, she decided that she wasn't just going to stand idly by. She decided to call the town's first public meeting about the AIDS crisis—something that no one had even talked about, let alone met about. Two hundred people showed up. Some had walked for miles to get there, a few with their grandchildren on their back.

One by one, they stood up and broke their silence, and they told their stories. Stories of tragedy, and stories of hope. And when they were done, Leo rose and said,

> "I don't know whether we will win this war, but I'm looking for people who will stand up and face the reality. The time for sitting silently has come to an end."

Everything did not suddenly get better after that meeting, but some things did. Despite all the children she had to raise and all the sick relatives she still had to care for, Leo still decided to open the AIDS orphanage she had dreamed about so long ago. She began building a daycare center that would house one hundred orphans. And she started plans on a youth center and a soup kitchen.

I hear that part of the story and I think, if this woman who has so little, and has lost so much, can do so much good—if she can still make a way out of no way—then what are we waiting for?

Corinthians says that we are all of one spirit, and that "if one part suffers, every part suffers with it." But it also says, "if one part is honored, every part rejoices with it."

On this World AIDS Day, it is the stories of overcoming, and not just illness, that the world needs to hear. Yes, the stories of sadness call us to suffer with the sick. But stories like Leo's also call us to honor her example, rejoice in the hope that it brings, and work to help her find that brighter future. Thank you, and God bless you.

POLITICS OF CHANGE
The Presidential Candidacy Speech
February 10, 2007

(Springfield, Illinois) Barack Obama delivered this speech, announcing his candidacy for the Presidency, taking as his theme the politics of change: *That is our unyielding faith—that in the face of impossible odds, people who love their country can change it.*

Let me begin by saying thanks to all you who've traveled, from far and wide, to brave the cold today. We all made this journey for a reason. It's humbling, but in my heart I know you didn't come here just for me, you came here because you believe in what this country can be. In the face of war, you believe there can be peace. In the face of despair, you believe there can be hope. In the face of a politics that's shut you out—that's told you to settle, that's divided us for too long—you believe we can be one people, reaching for what's possible, building that more perfect union.

That's the journey we're on today. But let me tell you how I came to be here. As most of you know, I am not a native of this great state. I moved to Illinois over two decades ago. I was a young man then, just a year out of college; I knew no one in Chicago, was without money or family connections. But a group of churches had offered me a job as a community organizer for $13,000 a year. And I accepted the job, sight unseen, motivated then by a single, simple, powerful idea—that I might play a small part in building a better America.

My work took me to some of Chicago's poorest neighborhoods. I joined with pastors and lay people to deal with communities that had been ravaged by plant closings. I saw that the problems people faced weren't simply local in nature—that the decision to close a steel mill was made by distant executives—that the lack of textbooks and computers in schools could be traced to the skewed priorities of politicians a thousand miles away, and that when a child turns to violence, there's a hole in his heart no government could ever fill.

It was in these neighborhoods that I received the best education I ever had, and where I learned the true meaning of my Christian faith.

After three years of this work, I went to law school, because I wanted to understand how the law should work for those in need. I became a civil rights lawyer, and taught constitutional law and, after a time, I came to understand that our cherished rights of liberty and equality depend on the active participation of an awakened electorate. It was with these ideas in mind that I arrived in this capital city as a state Senator.

It was here, in Springfield, where I saw all that is America converge—farmers and teachers, businessmen and laborers, all of them with a story to tell, all of them seeking a seat at the table, all of them clamoring to be heard....

It was here we learned to disagree without being disagreeable—that it's possible to compromise so long as you know those principles that can never be compromised, and that so long as we're willing to listen to each other, we can assume the best in people instead of the worst.

That's why we were able to reform a death penalty system that was broken. That's why we were able to give health insurance to children in need. That's why we made the tax system more fair and just for working families, and that's why we passed ethics reforms that the cynics said could never, ever be passed.

It was here, in Springfield ... that I was reminded of the essential decency of the American people—where I came to believe that through this decency we can build a more hopeful America.

And that is why, in the shadow of the Old State Capitol, where Lincoln once called on a divided house to stand together, ... I stand before you today to announce my candidacy for President of the United States.

I recognize there is a certain presumptuousness—a certain audacity—to this announcement. I know I haven't spent a lot of time learning the ways of Washington. But I've been there long enough to know that the ways of Washington must change.

The genius of our founders is that they designed a system of government that can be changed. And we should take heart, because we've changed this country before. In the face of tyranny, a band of patriots brought an Empire to its knees. In the face of secession, we unified a nation and set the captives free. In the face of Depression, we put people back to work and lifted millions out of poverty. We welcomed immigrants to our shores, we opened railroads to the west, we landed a man on the moon, and we heard a King's call to let justice roll down like water, and righteousness like a mighty stream.

Each and every time, a new generation has risen up and done what's needed to be done. Today we are called once more—and it is time for our generation to answer that call. For that is our unyielding faith—that in the face of impossible odds, people who love their country can change it.

That's what Abraham Lincoln understood. He had his doubts. He had his defeats. He had his setbacks. But through his will and his words, he moved a nation and helped free a people. It is because of the millions who rallied to his cause that we are no longer divided, North and South, slave and free. It is because men and women of every race, from every walk of life, continued to march for freedom long after Lincoln was laid to rest, that today we have the chance to face the challenges of this millennium together, as one people—as Americans.

All of us know what those challenges are today—a war with no end, a dependence on oil that threatens our future, schools where too many children aren't learning, and families struggling paycheck to paycheck despite working as hard as they can. We know the challenges. We've heard them. We've talked about them for years.

What's stopped us from meeting these challenges is not the absence of sound policies and sensible plans. What's stopped us is the failure of leadership, the smallness of our politics, the ease with which we're distracted by the petty and trivial, our chronic avoidance of tough decisions, our preference for scoring cheap political points instead of rolling up our sleeves and building a working consensus to tackle big problems.

For the last six years we've been told that our mounting debts don't matter, we've been told that the anxiety Americans feel about rising health care costs and stagnant wages are an illusion, we've been told that climate change is a hoax, and that tough talk and an ill-conceived war can replace diplomacy, and strategy, and foresight. And when all else fails—when Katrina happens, or the death toll in Iraq mounts—we've been told that our crises are somebody else's fault. We're distracted from our real failures, and told to blame the other party, or gay people, or immigrants.

And as people have looked away in disillusionment and frustration, we know what's filled the void. The cynics, and the lobbyists, and the special interests who've turned our government into a game only they can afford to play. They write the checks and you get stuck with the bills, they get the access while you get to write a letter, they think they own this government, but we're here today to take it back. The time for that politics is over. It's time to turn the page.

We've made some progress already.... But Washington has a long way to go. And it won't be easy. That's why we'll have to set priorities. We'll have to make hard choices. And although government will play a crucial role in bringing about the changes we need, more money and programs alone will not get us where we need to go. Each of us, in our own lives, will have to accept responsibility—for instilling an ethic of achievement in our children, for adapting to a more competitive economy, for strengthening our communities, and sharing some measure of sacrifice. So let us begin. Let us begin this hard work together. Let us transform this nation.

Let us be the generation that reshapes our economy to compete in the digital age. Let's set high standards for our schools and give them the resources they need to succeed. Let's recruit a new army of teachers, and give them better pay and more support in exchange for more accountability. Let's make college more affordable, and let's invest in scientific research, and let's lay down broadband lines through the heart of inner cities and rural towns all across America.

And as our economy changes, let's be the generation that ensures our nation's workers are sharing in our prosperity. Let's protect the hard-earned benefits their companies have promised. Let's make it possible for hardworking Americans to save for retirement. And let's allow our unions and their organizers to lift up this country's middle class again.

Let's be the generation that ends poverty in America. Every single person willing to work should be able to get job training that leads to a job, and earn a living wage that can pay the bills, and afford child care so their kids have a safe place to go when they work. Let's do this.

Let's be the generation that finally tackles our health care crisis. We can control costs by focusing on prevention, by providing better treatment to the chronically ill, and using technology to cut the bureaucracy. Let's be the generation that says right here, right now, that we will have universal health care in America by the end of the next president's first term.

Let's be the generation that finally frees America from the tyranny of oil. We can harness homegrown, alternative fuels like ethanol and spur the production of more fuel-efficient cars. We can set up a system for capping greenhouse gases. We can turn this crisis of global warming into a moment of opportunity for innovation, and job creation, and an incentive for businesses that will serve as a model for the world. Let's be the generation that makes future generations proud of what we did here.

Most of all, let's be the generation that never forgets what happened on that September day and confront the terrorists with everything we've got. Politics doesn't have to divide us on this anymore—we can work together to keep our country safe.... We can work together to track terrorists down with a stronger military, we can tighten the net around their finances, and we can improve our intelligence capabilities. But let us also understand that ultimate victory against our enemies will come only by rebuilding our alliances and exporting those ideals that bring hope and opportunity to millions around the globe.

But all of this cannot come to pass until we bring an end to this war in Iraq. Most of you know I opposed this war from the start. I thought it was a tragic mistake. Today we grieve for the families who have lost loved ones, the hearts that have been broken, and the young lives that could have been. America, it's time to start bringing our troops home. It's time to admit that no amount of American lives can resolve the political disagreement that lies at the heart of someone else's civil war. That's why I have a plan that will bring our combat troops home by March of 2008. Letting the Iraqis know that we will not be there forever is our last, best hope to pressure the Sunni and Shia to come to the table and find peace.

Finally, there is one other thing that is not too late to get right about this war, and that is the homecoming of the men and women—our veterans—who have sacrificed the most. Let us honor their valor by providing the care they need and rebuilding the military they love. Let us be the generation that begins this work.

I know there are those who don't believe we can do all these things. I understand the skepticism. After all, every four years, candidates from both parties make similar promises, and I expect this year will be no different. All of us running for president will travel around the country offering ten-point plans and making grand speeches. All of us will trumpet those qualities we believe make us uniquely qualified to lead the country. But too many times, after the election is over, and the confetti is swept away, all those promises fade from memory, and the lobbyists and the special interests move in, and people turn away, disappointed as before, left to struggle on their own.

That is why this campaign can't only be about me. It must be about us—it must be about what we can do together. This campaign must be the occasion, the vehicle, of your hopes, and your dreams. It will take your time, your energy, and your advice to push us forward when we're doing right, and to let us know when we're not. This campaign has to be about reclaiming the meaning of citizenship, restoring our sense of common purpose, and realizing that few obstacles can withstand the power of millions of voices calling for change.

By ourselves, this change will not happen. Divided, we are bound to fail.

But the life of a tall, gangly, self-made Springfield lawyer tells us that a different future is possible.

He tells us that there is power in words.

He tells us that there is power in conviction.

That beneath all the differences of race and region, faith and station, we are one people.

He tells us that there is power in hope.

As Lincoln organized the forces arrayed against slavery, he was heard to say, "Of strange, discordant, and even hostile elements, we gathered from the four winds, and formed and fought to battle through."

That is our purpose here today.

That's why I'm in this race. Not just to hold an office, but to gather with you to transform a nation.

I want to win that next battle—for justice and opportunity.

I want to win that next battle—for better schools, and better jobs, and health care for all.

I want us to take up the unfinished business of perfecting our union, and building a better America.

And if you will join me in this improbable quest, if you feel destiny calling, and see as I see, a future of endless possibility stretching before us—if you sense, as I sense, that the time is now to shake off our slumber, and slough off our fear, and make good on the debt we owe past and future generations—then I'm ready to take up the cause, and march with you, and work with you. Together, starting today, let us finish the work that needs to be done, and usher in a new birth of freedom on this Earth.

THIS IS NOT WHO WE ARE
The Health Care Crisis Speech
May 29, 2007

(Iowa City, Iowa) Barack Obama delivered this campaign speech at the University of Iowa, taking as his theme health care for the future: *Never forget that we have it within our power to shape history in this country. It is not in our character to sit idly by as victims of fate or circumstance, for we are a people of action and innovation, forever pushing the boundaries of what's possible.*

I want to give a special thanks to Amy and Lane for joining me today to tell their story.

A few hours north of here, Amy and Lane run a small business that offers internet service to their community. They were the very first company to provide broadband access in their remote corner of northeastern Iowa, and every day, hundreds of people count on the services they provide to do their jobs and live their lives.

But today they are on the brink of bankruptcy—a bankruptcy that has nothing to do with any poor business decision they made or slump in the economy they weren't prepared for. Lane was diagnosed with cancer when he was twenty-one years old. He lost a lung, a leg bone, and part of a hip. Seventeen years later, he is cancer-free, but the cost of health insurance for him, his wife, and his three kids is now over $1,000 per month. Their family's premiums keep rising hundreds of dollars every year and, as hard as they look, they simply cannot find another provider that will insure them.

Amy and Lane are now paying forty percent of their annual income in health care premiums. They have no retirement plan and nothing saved. They can no longer afford to buy new clothes or fill up their cars with gas, they have racked up more credit card debt then they know what to do with, and Amy wrote to us and said that the day she heard the loan officer say the word "bankruptcy" was one of the worst in her life.

"My heart was in pain," she said. "This is not who we are. We have done everything right. We have done everything we were supposed to do. This is not who we are."

Amy is right. This is not who we are. We are not a country that rewards hard work and perseverance with bankruptcies and foreclosures. We are not a country that allows major challenges to go unsolved and unaddressed while our people suffer needlessly. In the richest nation on Earth, it is simply not right that the skyrocketing profits of the drug and insurance industries are paid for by the skyrocketing premiums that come from the pockets of the American people.

This is not who we are. And this is not who we have to be.

In the past few months, I've heard stories like Amy's ... all across the country. Stories from people who are hanging on by a thread because of the stack of medical bills they can't pay. People who don't know where else to turn for help, but who do know that when it comes to health care, we have talked, tinkered, and let this crisis fester for decades. People who watch as every year candidates offer up detailed health care plans with great fanfare and promise, only to see them crushed under the weight of Washington politics and drug and insurance industry lobbying once the campaign is over.

Well, this cannot be one of those years. We have reached a point in this country where the rising cost of health care has put too many families and businesses on a collision course with financial ruin and left too many without coverage at all—a course that Democrats and Republicans, small business owners and CEOs, have all come to agree is not sustainable or acceptable any longer.

We often hear the statistic that there are 45 million uninsured Americans. But the biggest reason why they don't have insurance is the same reason why those who do have it are struggling to pay their medical bills—it's just too expensive.

Health care premiums have risen nearly 90% in the past six years. That's four times faster than wages have gone up. Like Amy and Lane's family, nearly half of all Iowans have said that they've had to cut back on food and heating expenses because of high health care costs. 11 million insured Americans spent more than a quarter of their salary on health care last year. And over half of all personal bankruptcies are now caused by medical bills.

Businesses aren't faring much better. Over half of all small businesses can no longer afford to insure their workers, and so many others have responded to rising costs by laying off workers or shutting their doors for good. Some of the biggest corporations in America, giants of industry like GM and Ford, are watching foreign competitors based in countries with universal health care run circles around them, with a GM car containing seven times as much health care cost as a Japanese car.

This cost crisis is trapping us in a vicious cycle. As premiums rise, more employers drop coverage, and more Americans become uninsured. Every time those uninsured walk into an emergency room and receive care that's more expensive because they have nowhere else to turn, there is a hidden tax for the rest of us as premiums go up by an extra $922 per family. And as premiums keep rising, more families and businesses drop their coverage and become uninsured.

It would be one thing if all this money we spend on premiums and co-payments and deductibles went directly towards making us healthier and improving the quality of our care. But it doesn't. One out of every four dollars we spend on health care is swallowed up by administrative costs—on needless paperwork and antiquated recordkeeping that belongs in the last century. This failure to update the way our doctors and hospitals store and share information also leads to costly errors. Each year 100,000 Americans die due to medical errors and we lose $100 billion because of prescription drug errors alone.

We also spend far more on treating illnesses and conditions that could've been prevented or managed for far less. Our health care system is turning into a disease care system, where too many plans and providers don't offer or encourage check-ups and tests and screenings that could save thousands of lives and billions of dollars down the road.

Of course, the biggest obstacle in the way of reforming this skewed system of needless waste and spiraling costs are those who profit most from the status quo—the drug and insurance companies who pocket a growing chunk of the medical bills that people like Amy and Lane are going bankrupt trying to pay.

Since President Bush took office, the single fastest growing component of health care spending has been administrative costs and profits for insurance companies. Coming in a close second is the amount we spend on prescription drugs. In 2006, five of the biggest drug and insurance companies were among the fifty most profitable businesses in the nation. One insurance company CEO received a $125 million salary that same year, and has been given stock options worth over $1 billion. As an added perk, he and his wife get free private health care for as long as they live.

Now, making this kind of money costs money, which is why the drug and insurance industries have also spent more than $1 billion on lobbying and campaign contributions over the last ten years to block the kind of reform we need. They've been pretty good at it too, preventing the sale of cheaper prescription drugs and defeating attempts to make it harder for insurance companies to deny coverage on the basis of a preexisting condition.

Look, it's perfectly understandable for a business to try and make a profit, and every American has the right to make their case to the people who represent us in Washington. But I also believe that every American has the right to affordable health care. I believe that the millions of Americans who can't take their children to a doctor when they get sick have that right. I believe that people like Amy and Lane who are on the brink of losing everything they own have that right. And I believe that no amount of industry profiteering and lobbying should stand in the way of that right any longer.

That's not who we are.

We now face an opportunity—and an obligation—to turn the page on the failed politics of yesterday's health care debates. It's time to bring together businesses, the medical community, and members of both parties around a comprehensive solution to this crisis, and it's time to let the drug and insurance industries know that, while they'll get a seat at the table, they don't get to buy every chair.

We can do this. The climate is far different than it was the last time we tried this in the early nineties. Since then, rising costs have caused many more businesses to back reform, and in states from Massachusetts to California, Democratic and Republican governors and legislatures have been way ahead of Washington in passing increasingly bolder initiatives to cover the uninsured and cut costs.

…. It's a goal I believe we can achieve on a national level with the health care plan I'm outlining today. The very first promise I made on this campaign was that, as president, I will sign a universal health care plan into law by the end of my first term in office. Today I want to lay out the details of that plan—a plan that not only guarantees coverage for every American, but also brings down the cost of health care and reduces every family's premiums by as much as $2500. This second part is important because, in the end, coverage without cost containment will only shift our burdens, not relieve them. So we will take steps to remove the waste and inefficiency from the system so we can bring down costs and improve the quality of our care while we're at it.

My plan begins by covering every American.

If you already have health insurance, the only thing that will change for you under this plan is the amount of money you will spend on premiums. That will be less.

If you are one of the 45 million Americans who don't have health insurance, you will have it after this plan becomes law. No one will be turned away because of a preexisting condition or illness. Everyone will be able buy into a new health insurance plan that's similar to the one that every federal employee—from a postal worker in Iowa to a Congressman in Washington—currently has for themselves. It will cover all essential medical services, including preventive, maternity, disease management, and mental health care. And it will also include high standards for quality and efficiency.

If you cannot afford this insurance, you will receive a subsidy to pay for it. If you have children, they will be covered. If you change jobs, your insurance will go with you. If you need to see a doctor, you will not have to wait in long lines for one. If you want more choices, you will also have the option of purchasing a number of affordable private plans that have similar benefits and standards for quality and efficiency.

To help pay for this, we will ask all but the smallest businesses who don't make a meaningful contribution today to the health coverage of their employees to do so by supporting this new plan. And we will allow the temporary Bush tax cut for the wealthiest Americans to expire.

But we also have to demand greater efficiencies from our health care system. Today, we pay almost twice as much for health care per person than other industrialized nations, and too much of it has nothing to do with patient care.

That's why the second part of my health care plan includes five, long-overdue steps we will take to bring down costs and bring our health care system into the 21st century....

First, we will reduce costs for business and their workers by picking up the tab for some of the most expensive illnesses and conditions.

Right now, two out of every ten patients account for more than eighty percent of all health care costs. These are patients with serious illnesses like cancer or heart disease who require the most expensive surgeries and treatments. Insurance companies end up spending a lion's share of their expenses on these patients and, not surprisingly, they pass those expenses on to the rest of us in the form of higher premiums. Under my proposal, the federal government will pay for part of these catastrophic cases, which means that your premiums will go down.

Second, we will finally begin focusing our health care system on preventing costly, debilitating conditions in the first place.

We all know the saying that an ounce of prevention is worth a pound of cure. But today we're nowhere close to that ounce. We spend less than four cents of every health care dollar on prevention and public health even though eighty percent of the risk factors involved in the leading causes of death are behavior-related and thus preventable.

The problem is, there's currently no financial incentive for health care providers to offer services that will encourage patients to eat right or exercise or go for annual check-ups and screenings that can help detect diseases early. The real profit today is made in treating diseases, not preventing them. That's wrong, which is why in our new national health care plan and other participating plans, we will require coverage of evidence-based, preventive care services, and make sure they are paid for. But in the end, prevention only works if we take responsibility for our own health and make the right decisions in our own lives—if we eat the right foods, and stay active, and listen to our wives when they tell us to stop smoking.

Third, we will reduce the cost of our health care by improving the quality of our health care.

It's estimated that poor quality care currently costs us up to $100 billion a year. One study found that in Pennsylvania, Medicare spent $1 billion a year just on treating infections that patients contracted while at the hospital—infections that could have easily been prevented.... This study led hospitals across the state to take action, and today some have completely eliminated infections that used to take hundreds of lives and cost hundreds of thousands of dollars every year.

... [My] health care proposal will ask hospitals and providers to collect, track, and publicly report measures of health care quality. We'll provide the public with information about preventable medical errors, nurse-to-patient ratios, and hospital-acquired infections. We'll also start measuring what's effective and what's not when it comes to different drugs and procedures, so that patients can finally start making informed choices about the care that's best for them. And instead of rewarding providers and physicians only by the sheer quantity of services and procedures they prescribe, we'll start rewarding them for the quality of the outcomes for their patients.

Fourth, we will reduce waste and inefficiency by moving from a 20th century health care industry based on pen and paper to a 21st century industry based on the latest information technology.

Almost every other industry in the world has saved billions on administrative costs by computerizing all of their records and information. Every transaction you make at a bank now costs less than a dollar. Even at the Veterans Administration, where it used to cost nine dollars to pull up your medical record, new technology means you can call up the same record on the internet for next to nothing. But because we haven't updated technology in the rest of the health care industry, a single transaction still costs up to twenty-five dollars.

This reform is long overdue. By moving to electronic medical records, we can give doctors and nurses easy access to all the necessary information about their patients, so if they type in a certain prescription, a patient's allergies will pop right up on the screen. This will reduce deadly medical errors, and it will also shorten the length of hospital stays, ensure that nurses can spend less time on paperwork and more time with patients, and save billions and billions of dollars in the process.

Finally, we will break the stranglehold that a few big drug and insurance companies have on the health care market.

We all value the medical cures and innovations that the pharmaceutical industry has developed over the years, but it's become clear that some of these companies are dramatically overcharging Americans for what they offer. They'll sell the same exact drugs here in America for double the price of what they charge in Europe and Canada. They'll push expensive products on doctors by showering them with gifts, spend more to market and advertise their drugs than to research and develop them, and when a generic drug maker comes along and wants to sell the same product for cheaper, the brand-name manufacturers will actually pay off the generic ones so they can preserve their monopolies and keep charging the rest of us high prices.

We don't have to stand for that anymore. Under my plan, we will make generic drugs more available to consumers and we will tell the drug companies that their days of forcing affordable prescription drugs out of the market are over.

And it's not just the drug industry that's manipulating the market. In the last ten years, there have been over four hundred health insurance mergers. Right here in Iowa, just three companies control more than three-quarters of the health insurance market. These changes were supposed to increase efficiency in the industry. But what's really increased is the amount of money we're paying them.

This is wrong, and when I'm President, we're going to make drug and insurance companies compete for their customers just like every other business in America. We'll investigate and prosecute the monopolization of the insurance industry. And where we do find places where insurance companies aren't competitive, we will make them pay a reasonable share of their profits on the patients they should be caring for in the first place. Because that's what's right.

We are a country that looks at the thousands of stories just like Amy and Lane's—stories we have heard and told for decades—and realizes that our American story calls on us to write them a hopeful, happier ending. After all, that's what we've done before.

Half a century ago, America found itself in the midst of another health care crisis. For millions of elderly Americans, the single greatest cause of poverty and hardship was the crippling cost of their health care. A third of all elderly Americans lived in poverty, and nearly half had no health insurance. As health care and hospital costs continued to rise, more and more private insurers simply refused to insure our elderly, believing they were too great of a risk to care for.

The resistance to action was fierce. Proponents of health care reform were opposed by well-financed, well-connected interest groups who spared no expense in telling the American people that these efforts were "dangerous" and "un-American," "revolutionary" and even "deadly." And yet the reformers marched on. They testified before Congress and they took their case to the country and they introduced dozens of different proposals but always, always they stood firm on their goal to provide affordable health care for every American senior. And finally, after years of advocacy and negotiation and plenty of setbacks, President Lyndon Johnson signed the Medicare bill into law on July 30th of 1965. The signing ceremony was held in Missouri, in a town called Independence, with the man who issued the call for universal health care during his own presidency—Harry Truman. And as he stood with Truman by his side and signed what would become one of the most successful government programs in history—a program that had seemed impossible for so long—President Johnson looked out at the crowd and said, "History shapes men, but it is a necessary faith of leadership that men can help shape history."

Never forget that we have it within our power to shape history in this country. It is not in our character to sit idly by as victims of fate or circumstance, for we are a people of action and innovation, forever pushing the boundaries of what's possible.

Now is the time to push those boundaries once more. We have come so far in the debate on health care in this country, but now we must finally answer the call issued by Truman, advanced by Johnson, and pushed along by the simple power of stories like the one told by Amy and Lane. The time has come for affordable, universal health care in America. And I look forward to working with all of you to meet this challenge in the weeks and months to come.

STRENGTHENING FAMILIES
The New Economy Speech
June 15, 2007

(Spartanburg, South Carolina) Barack Obama delivered this campaign speech at the Mount Moriah Baptist Church, taking as his theme individual and collective responsibility in the new economy: *For the families who've been hit hardest by these economic changes, we have to help them get started before we can help them get ahead—we have to empower them to grab that first rung of the ladder before they start climbing.*

Each year at this time we honor and think about the fathers who've been a part of our lives—the examples they've set, the sacrifices they've made, their successes and their struggles.

I think about my grandfather, who first became a father when my mother was born on a Kansas army base at the outset of World War II. He left to fight fascism in Europe while my grandmother stayed behind and pitched in on a bomber assembly line. With the nation still dragging itself out of Depression, I imagine he must have felt uncertain at that time about what the future held for his family, and yet he returned to a country newly committed to opportunity—a country that gave him a chance to go to college on the GI Bill, buy a house thanks to the Federal Housing Authority, and move west to Hawaii to raise his family.

I also think about my father-in-law, Fraser Robinson. He raised his two children with his wife Marian in 1960s Chicago. They faced what other African-American families faced at the time—both hidden and overt forms of racism that limited their opportunities and required more effort to get ahead. And they faced an additional obstacle. At age 30, Fraser was diagnosed with multiple sclerosis. And yet, every day of his life, even when he had to rely on a walker to get him there, he went to work at the local water filtration plant while Marian stayed home with the children. And on that single salary, Fraser Robinson provided for his family, sending my wife Michelle and her brother Craig to Princeton.

And of course, though I did not know him well, every year around Father's Day I think of my own father. He and my mother divorced when I was only two years old, and for most of my life I knew him only through the letters he sent and the stories my mother and grandparents told.

In his absence, it was more difficult for my mother to raise me and my sister on one salary during the 1970s, and we struggled, at times turning to food stamps to get us through the month. And yet, through the support of my grandparents, the sheer will and determination of my mother, and the blessings of generous scholarships, I was able to attend some of the best schools in the country—schools that made it possible for me to stand here today.

It has not been lost on either Michelle or myself that our family's story has been America's story—a story of opportunity, and possibility, and the tireless pursuit of a dream that was always within reach. Our parents and grandparents were given no guarantees, and they certainly had their share of failings and hardship, but theirs was a country where if you wanted it badly enough, and were willing to work for it, and take responsibility, you could provide for your family and give your children the same chance.

There are fewer and fewer families who can tell this story today. Unlike my grandfather, the brave soldiers who return from Iraq and Afghanistan are lucky if they come home to a job that pays the bills, or even the benefits and care they've earned as veterans. Blue-collar workers like Fraser Robinson have seen their benefits decline, and their unions weakened, and their wages flattened, while the cost of everything else rises. And as many of you know too well, single parents no longer have the support system that my mother did, with too many fathers financially unable to help raise their children even if they want to do the right thing.

Over the last few decades, fundamental changes in the way we work and live have trapped too many American families between an economy that's gone global and a government that's gone AWOL. Too many rungs have been removed from the ladder to middle-class security, and the safety net that's supposed to break any falls from that ladder has grown badly frayed. Many families face increased anxiety when it comes to paying the bills or finding ways to spend more time with their children, while others have tumbled into poverty, watching jobs disappear, and fathers leave the home. And even though the vast majority of mothers are now working—including single mothers—we haven't yet provided them with the support they need to raise their children.

I don't have to give you a history lesson in economics for you to know how this all happened, because many of you have seen it or even lived it. You've seen the factories close their doors and move overseas, leaving too many cities and mill towns without their biggest source of employment. I saw it when I first arrived in Chicago in the early 80s, where I took a job helping to rebuild neighborhoods that had been devastated by steel plant closings.

And today, it's not just factory jobs that are disappearing. As countries like China and India churn out more workers who are educated longer and better, revolutions in technology and communication have made it possible for American companies to automate some jobs and send others wherever there's an internet connection.

The jobs that remain pay less and offer fewer benefits, as employers have succeeded in busting up unions and cutting back on health care and pensions to stay competitive with the companies abroad that are paying their workers next to nothing.

The weekly earnings of American workers, which had steadily risen during the years our parents and grandparents were employed, have fallen more than twenty percent since 1973, and the minimum wage hasn't moved in ten years. This means that right now, a family of three with one minimum-wage earner is still more than $6000 below the poverty line.

Most Americans are vulnerable to these new risks, but without a doubt the hardest hit have been those families who were most vulnerable to begin with. They are families who live in inner-cities and remote rural areas; they are disproportionately African-American and Latino.

In the last six years, over 300,000 black males have lost jobs in the manufacturing sector—the highest rate of any ethnic group. In urban areas, more than 50% of black men do not complete high school. In one survey, nearly one out of every three African-American families said they experienced at least one of three hardships in the last year—overcrowded housing, a lack of medical care, or hunger. Without a job or an education, many black men simply cannot afford to raise a family—and too many have made the sad choice not to. Today, 54% of all African-American children live in single-parent households, a number that has doubled since 1960. Now, many single moms—including the one who raised me—do a heroic job on behalf of their kids. But in an economy where a two-income family has become a financial necessity, a fatherless household takes its toll. Children who grow up without a father are five times more likely to live in poverty and nine times more likely to drop out of school.

Providing these families with the same chances that previous generations have had is a daunting challenge, but it is certainly one we can meet.

.... [We] know what needs to be done when it comes to giving our families a fighting chance. And I think it's time we finally had a President who gets Washington to start doing it. I don't know about you, but I'm tired of hearing that town tell us we can't. For too long, they've told us we can't do anything about disappearing jobs and stagnant wages. They've told us that we can't lower our health care costs or the price of college tuition. They've told us that poverty is a nuisance to blame on the impoverished, not a moral shame that should outrage a nation. We're assured that the market will correct all our misfortunes, and that there's no problem that can't be solved by another tax break that the wealthy didn't need and didn't ask for.

Well, we have tried it their way for six years and we're ready to try something new. It's time to turn the page.

We are not a country that settles for survival of the fittest, but a people who have always fought for survival of the nation. That's how we got a GI Bill that sent a generation to college and created the largest middle class in history. That's how we gave workers the right to organize and form a union. That's how we got Social Security and Medicare, so that Americans could retire in comfort and dignity.

Now we have to do it again. And it won't be easy. We know that we can't put the forces of globalization back in the bottle. We cannot bring back every job that's been lost. We have to find a way to make this new economy work for us.

We also know that government cannot meet this challenge alone—that there is not a program for every problem we face. It will take responsibility and sacrifice from the American people; changes in habits and attitudes. We will need to work more, read more, train more, and think more. Parents will need to make sure their kids turn off the TV once in a while, and put away the video games, and start hitting the books. And there are a lot of men out there who need to stop acting like boys, who need to realize that responsibility does not end at conception, who need to know that what makes you a man is not the ability to have a child but the courage to raise one.

But just as we have individual responsibilities, at the dawn of the 21st century we also have a collective responsibility to strengthen that safety net, put the rungs back on that ladder to the middle class, and give every family the chance that so many of our parents and grandparents had. This responsibility is one that's been missing from Washington for far too long—a responsibility I intend to take very seriously as President.

We know what we need to do to help every family compete and prosper in a globalized world. We know that we need to invest in the science and technology that will make America the home for the high-tech, high-wage jobs of tomorrow.

We know that to fill these jobs, we'll also have to get serious about educating our workforce for the 21st century. This means starting our kids in school younger, with more early childhood education opportunities.... It means improving our public schools by recruiting thousands of new teachers and paying them more and asking more of them. And it means making college affordable for every American who wants to go by offering more loans and bigger grants.

And of course, in a world of increased risks and insecurities, we also know that every American needs a health care plan and a retirement plan that stays with them no matter where they work or even if they can't find work....

So we know that we need this broader agenda to help families get ahead in this new world. But we also know that for the families who've been hit hardest by these economic changes, we have to help them get started before we can help them get ahead—we have to empower them to grab that first rung of the ladder before they start climbing. That's why today I want to lay out a plan that would strengthen some of our most vulnerable families by ensuring that they can find a job, stay out of poverty, and get the support they need to raise their children.

First, we need to ensure that everyone who is willing to work can find a job.... [This] certainly isn't easy. But it's a promise we have to keep in this country.

So, for those Americans who have been searching unsuccessfully for employment, I will invest $50 million in programs that will place willing workers into transitional jobs and train them for permanent ones.

These programs have already proven to be highly successful in the many communities that have tried them. People get the chance to work in a community service-type job, earn a paycheck every week, and learn the skills they need for gainful employment. And by leaving with references and a resume, oftentimes they find that employment.

.... [We'll] also work with community organizations and businesses to create career pathways that provide workers with the additional skills and training they need to earn more money and keep climbing up that ladder to middle-class security. Unions and various communities have done this quite successfully, and this program would build on that model.

The second step we'll take to strengthen families is to ensure that working Americans are not impoverished Americans.

One of the most successful anti-poverty programs in history has been the Earned Income Tax Credit—additional income that lifts nearly 5 million Americans out of poverty every year. As President, I will double the number of single workers who receive the EITC and triple the benefit for full-time workers making the minimum wage, from the $175 they get today to $555. And instead of waiting every ten years for Congress to fight over raising the minimum wage, I will finally make the minimum wage a living wage by permanently indexing it to inflation so that it actually pays the bills.

The third step we'll take to strengthen families is to give them the support they need to raise their children.

As President, I'll start by passing the plan I outlined last year that would make it easier for fathers who make the responsible choice and harder for those who avoid it. It's a plan that would remove some of the financial penalties the government currently imposes on married couples, cut out the red tape to ensure that every dime of child support goes directly to children instead of bureaucrats, and provide fathers who are paying their child support an even larger EITC benefit. This plan would also crack down on those who avoid their responsibility by increasing child-support enforcement, a measure that will collect nearly $13 billion in payments that can help raise, nurture, and educate children.

We should also help new mothers with their new responsibilities. There is a pioneering Nurse-Family Partnership program right now that offers home visits by trained registered nurses to low-income mothers and mothers-to-be. They learn how to care for themselves before the baby is born and what to do after. They are counseled on substance abuse, creating and achieving personal goals, and effective methods of nurturing children. Where it's been tried, this program reduced childhood injuries and unintended pregnancies, increased father involvement and women's employment, reduced use of welfare and food stamps, and increased children's school readiness. And it produced more than $28,000 in net savings for every high-risk family enrolled in the program. As President, I will expand the Nurse-Family Partnership to provide at-home nurse visits for up to 570,000 first-time mothers each year.

My plan would also support families with children by expanding the Child Tax Credit to an additional 600,000 more Americans, who would receive $1,000 per child. And for all those families where both parents work and don't know what to do when their child has to stay home sick for the day, my plan guarantees every worker seven paid days of sick leave each year.

None of this agenda will happen overnight, nor will it be easy to get done. But then again, America's story hasn't been all that easy itself. It is filled with tales of those who risked and struggled and beat the odds because they knew that this is a place—perhaps the only place—where such triumph is always possible. Because they believe that the pursuit of happiness is not just a phrase in a declaration, but the founding promise of our country—a promise that sustained our parents and grandparents through war and depression, racial and social strife, heartache and hardship.

It's a promise that sustains this generation still.

The other day we heard from a young man named Joshua Stroman who's from right here in South Carolina. Joshua never knew his father, and when he was very young, his mom and stepfather both died from cancer. He was then taken in by family members who were involved with gangs and drugs. He experimented with that lifestyle for a bit, and his low point came when he went to jail at eighteen years old.

That's when he decided that his story would have a different ending. He began to find comfort in his faith, and when he left jail, he moved in with an aunt who expected him to behave well and study hard. And he did. He is now at Benedict College and will be president of the student council there next year. But he told us that of everything that's out there, his biggest dream is to someday stand in the front yard of his own home with his wife and kids, who will hug him and say, "I love you, Daddy."

It's a dream that could not be simpler or more profound—a dream that, in some form or another, has probably animated the journey that so many fathers and mothers and young men like Josh have taken over the generations. He has turned his life around because he held close the belief that it was always within reach. Now it is our task to turn this country around so that we can prove to him and so many others that they were right all along. I look forward to working with all of you in making this happen.

POLITICS OF CONSCIENCE
The Common Destiny Speech
June 23, 2007

(Hartford, Connecticut) Barack Obama delivered this campaign speech at the Synod of the United Church of Christ, taking as his theme the politics of conscience: *If we can embrace a common destiny—then I believe we'll not just help bring about a more hopeful day in America, we'll not just be caring for our own souls, we'll be doing God's work here on Earth.*

It's been several months now since I announced I was running for president. In that time, I've had the chance to talk with Americans all across this country. And I've found that no matter where I am, or who I'm talking to, there's a common theme that emerges. It's that folks are hungry for change—they're hungry for something new. They're ready to turn the page on the old politics and the old policies—whether it's the war in Iraq or the health care crisis we're in, or a school system that's leaving too many kids behind despite the slogans.

But I also get the sense that there's a hunger that's deeper than that—a hunger that goes beyond any single cause or issue. It seems to me that each day, thousands of Americans are going about their lives—dropping the kids off at school, driving to work, shopping at the mall, trying to stay on their diets, trying to kick a cigarette habit—and they're coming to the realization that something is missing. They're deciding that their work, their possessions, their diversions, their sheer busyness, is not enough.

They want a sense of purpose, a narrative arc to their lives. They're looking to relieve a chronic loneliness. And so they need an assurance that somebody out there cares about them, is listening to them—that they are not just destined to travel down that long road toward nothingness.

And this restlessness—this search for meaning—is familiar to me. I was not raised in a particularly religious household. My father, who I didn't know, returned to Kenya when I was just two. He was nominally a Muslim since there were a number of Muslims in the village where he was born. But by the time he was a young adult, he was an atheist. My mother, whose parents were non-practicing Baptists and Methodists, was one of the most spiritual souls I ever knew. She had this enormous capacity for wonder, and lived by the Golden Rule. But she had a healthy skepticism of religion as an institution. And as a consequence, so did I.

It wasn't until after college, when I went to Chicago to work as a community organizer for a group of Christian churches, that I confronted my own spiritual dilemma. In a sense, what brought me to Chicago in the first place was a hunger for some sort of meaning in my life. I wanted to be part of something larger. I'd been inspired by the civil rights movement—by all the clear-eyed, straight-backed, courageous young people who'd boarded buses and traveled down South to march and sit at lunch counters, and lay down their lives in some cases for freedom. I was too young to be involved in that movement, but I felt I could play a small part in the continuing battle for justice by helping rebuild some of Chicago's poorest neighborhoods.

So it's 1985, and I'm in Chicago, and I'm working with these churches, and with lots of laypeople who are much older than I am. And I found that I recognized in these folks a part of myself. I learned that everyone's got a sacred story when you take the time to listen. And I think they recognized a part of themselves in me too. They saw that I knew the Scriptures and that many of the values I held and that propelled me in my work were values they shared. But I think they also sensed that a part of me remained removed and detached—that I was an observer in their midst.

And slowly, I came to realize that something was missing as well—that without an anchor for my beliefs, without a commitment to a particular community of faith, at some level I would always remain apart, and alone. And it's around this time that some pastors I was working with came up to me and asked if I was a member of a church. "If you're organizing churches," they said, "it might be helpful if you went to church once in a while." And I thought, "Well, I guess that makes sense."

So one Sunday, I put on one of the few clean jackets I had, and went over to Trinity United Church of Christ on 95th Street on the South Side of Chicago. And I heard Reverend Jeremiah A. Wright deliver a sermon called "The Audacity of Hope." And during the course of that sermon, he introduced me to someone named Jesus Christ. I learned that my sins could be redeemed. I learned that those things I was too weak to accomplish myself, He would accomplish with me if I placed my trust in Him. And in time, I came to see faith as more than just a comfort to the weary or a hedge against death, but rather as an active, palpable agent in the world and in my own life.

It was because of these newfound understandings that I was finally able to walk down the aisle of Trinity one day and affirm my Christian faith. It came about as a choice, and not an epiphany. I didn't fall out in church, as folks sometimes do. The questions I had didn't magically disappear. The skeptical bent of my mind didn't suddenly vanish. But kneeling beneath that cross on the South Side, I felt I heard God's spirit beckoning me. I submitted myself to His will, and dedicated myself to discovering His truth and carrying out His works.

But my journey is part of a larger journey—one shared by all who've ever sought to apply the values of their faith to our society. It's a journey that takes us back to our nation's founding, when none other than a UCC [United Church of Christ] church inspired the Boston Tea Party and helped bring an Empire to its knees. In the following century, men and women of faith waded into the battles over prison reform and temperance, public education and women's rights and, above all, abolition. And when the Civil War was fought and our country dedicated itself to a new birth of freedom, they took on the problems of an industrializing nation—fighting the crimes against society and the sins against God that they felt were being committed in our factories and in our slums.

And when these battles were overtaken by others and when the wars they opposed were waged and won, these faithful foot soldiers for justice kept marching. They stood on the Edmund Pettus Bridge, as the blows of billy clubs rained down. They held vigils across this country when four little girls were killed in the 16th Street Baptist Church. They cheered on the steps of the Lincoln Memorial when Dr. King delivered his prayer for our country. And in all these ways, they helped make this country more decent and more just.

So doing the Lord's work is a thread that's run through our politics since the very beginning. And it puts the lie to the notion that the separation of church and state in America means faith should have no role in public life. Imagine Lincoln's Second Inaugural without its reference to "the judgments of the Lord." Or King's "I Have a Dream" speech without its reference to "all of God's children." Or President Kennedy's Inaugural without the words, "here on Earth, God's work must truly be our own." At each of these junctures, by summoning a higher truth and embracing a universal faith, our leaders inspired ordinary people to achieve extraordinary things.

But somehow, somewhere along the way, faith stopped being used to bring us together and started being used to drive us apart. It got hijacked. Part of it's because of the so-called leaders of the Christian Right, who've been all too eager to exploit what divides us. At every opportunity, they've told evangelical Christians that Democrats disrespect their values and dislike their Church, while suggesting to the rest of the country that religious Americans care only about issues like abortion and gay marriage; school prayer and intelligent design. There was even a time when the Christian Coalition determined that its number one legislative priority was tax cuts for the rich. I don't know what Bible they're reading, but it doesn't jibe with my version.

But I'm hopeful because I think there's an awakening taking place in America. People are coming together around a simple truth—that we are all connected, that I am my brother's keeper; I am my sister's keeper. And that it's not enough to just believe this—we have to do our part to make it a reality. My faith teaches me that I can sit in church and pray all I want, but I won't be fulfilling God's will unless I go out and do the Lord's work.

That's why pastors ... and organizations like World Vision and Catholic Charities are wielding their enormous influence to confront poverty, HIV/AIDS, and the genocide in Darfur. Religious leaders ... are working for justice and fighting for change. And all across the country, communities of faith are sponsoring day care programs, building senior centers, and in so many other ways, taking part in the project of American renewal.

Yet what we also understand is that our values should express themselves not just through our churches or synagogues, temples or mosques; they should express themselves through our government. Because whether it's poverty or racism, the uninsured or the unemployed, war or peace, the challenges we face today are not simply technical problems in search of the perfect ten-point plan. They are moral problems, rooted in both societal indifference and individual callousness—in the imperfections of man.

And so long as we're not doing everything in our personal and collective power to solve them, we know the conscience of our nation cannot rest.

Our conscience can't rest so long as 37 million Americans are poor and forgotten by their leaders in Washington and by the media elites. We need to heed the biblical call to care for "the least of these" and lift the poor out of despair.... If you're working forty hours a week, you shouldn't be living in poverty. But we also know that government initiatives are not enough. Each of us in our own lives needs to do what we can to help the poor. And until we do, our conscience cannot rest.

Our conscience cannot rest so long as nearly 45 million Americans don't have health insurance and the millions more who do are going bankrupt trying to pay for it. I have made a solemn pledge that I will sign a universal health care bill into law by the end of my first term as president that will cover every American and cut the cost of a typical family's premiums by up to $2500 a year. That's not simply a matter of policy or ideology— it's a moral commitment.

And until we stop the genocide that's being carried out in Darfur as I speak, our conscience cannot rest. This is a problem that's brought together churches and synagogues and mosques and people of all faiths as part of a grassroots movement. Universities and states, including Illinois, are taking part in a divestment campaign to pressure the Sudanese government to stop the killings. It's not enough, but it's helping. And it's a testament to what we can achieve when good people with strong convictions stand up for their beliefs.

And we should close Guantanamo Bay and stop tolerating the torture of our enemies. Because it's not who we are. It's not consistent with our traditions of justice and fairness. And it offends our conscience.

But we also know our conscience cannot rest so long as the war goes on in Iraq. It's a war I'm proud I opposed from the start—a war that should never have been authorized and never been waged. I have a plan that would have already begun redeploying our troops with the goal of bringing all our combat brigades home by March 31st of next year. The President vetoed a similar plan, but he doesn't have the last word, and we're going to keep at it, until we bring this war to an end. Because the Iraq war is not just a security problem, it's a moral problem.

And there's another issue we must confront as well. Today there are 12 million undocumented immigrants in America, most of them working in our communities, attending our churches, and contributing to our country.

Now, as children of God, we believe in the worth and dignity of every human being; it doesn't matter where that person came from or what documents they have. We believe that everyone, everywhere, should be loved, and given the chance to work and raise a family.

But as Americans, we also know that this is a nation of laws, and we cannot have those laws broken when more than 2,000 people cross our borders illegally every day. We cannot ignore that we have a right and a duty to protect our borders. And we cannot ignore the very real concerns of Americans who are not worried about illegal immigration because they are racist or xenophobic, but because they fear it will result in lower wages when they're already struggling to raise their families.... Our conscience cannot rest until we not only secure our borders, but give the 12 million undocumented immigrants in this country a chance to earn their citizenship by paying a fine and waiting in line behind all those who came here legally. We will all have to make concessions to achieve this. That's what compromise is about. But at the end of the day, we cannot walk away—not for the sake of passing a bill, but so that we can finally address the real concerns of Americans and the persistent hopes of all those brothers and sisters who want nothing more than their own chance at our common dream.

These are some of the challenges that test our conscience—as Americans and people of faith. And meeting them won't be easy. There is real evil and hardship and pain and suffering in the world and we should be humble in our belief that we can eliminate them. But we shouldn't use our humility as an excuse for inaction. We shouldn't use the obstacles we face as an excuse for cynicism. We have to do what we can, knowing it's hard and not swinging from a naïve idealism to a bitter defeatism but, rather, accepting the fact that we're not going to solve every problem overnight, but we can still make a difference.

We can recognize the truth that's at the heart of the UCC—that the conversation is not over, that our roles are not defined, that through ancient texts and modern voices, God is still speaking, challenging us to change not just our own lives, but the world around us.

I'm hearing from evangelicals who may not agree with progressives on every issue but agree that poverty has no place in a world of plenty, that hate has no place in the hearts of believers, and that we all have to be good stewards of God's creations. From Willow Creek to the 'emerging church,' from the Southern Baptist Convention to the National Association of Evangelicals, folks are realizing that the four walls of the church are too small for a big God. God is still speaking.

I'm hearing from progressives who understand that if we want to communicate our hopes and values to Americans, we can't abandon the field of religious discourse. That's why organizations are rising up across the country to reclaim the language of faith to bring about change. God is still speaking.

He's still speaking to our Catholic friends—who are holding up a consistent ethic of life that goes beyond abortion—one that includes a respect for life and dignity whether it's in Iraq, in poor neighborhoods, in African villages or even on death row. They're telling me that their conversation about what it means to be Catholic continues. God is still speaking.

And right here in the UCC, we're hearing from God about what it means to be a welcoming church that holds on to our Christian witness. The UCC is still listening. And God is still speaking.

Now, some of you may have heard me talk about the Joshua generation. But there's a story I want to share that takes place before Moses passed the mantle of leadership on to Joshua. It comes from Deuteronomy 30 when Moses talks to his followers about the challenges they'll find when they reach the Promised

Land without him. To the Joshua generation, these challenges seem momentous—and they are. But Moses says—What I am commanding you is not too difficult for you or beyond your reach. It is not up in heaven. Nor is it beyond the sea. No, the word is very near. It is on your lips and in your heart.

It's an idea that's often forgotten or dismissed in cynical times. It's that we all have it within our power to make this a better world. Because we all have the capacity to do justice and show mercy, to treat others with dignity and respect, and to rise above what divides us and come together to meet those challenges we can't meet alone. It's the wisdom Moses imparted to those who would succeed him. And it's a lesson we need to remember today, as members of another Joshua generation.

So let's rededicate ourselves to a new kind of politics—a politics of conscience. Let's come together—Protestant and Catholic, Muslim and Hindu and Jew, believer and non-believer alike. We're not going to agree on everything, but we can disagree without being disagreeable. We can affirm our faith without endangering the separation of church and state, as long as we understand that when we're in the public square, we have to speak in universal terms that everyone can understand. And if we can do that—if we can embrace a common destiny—then I believe we'll not just help bring about a more hopeful day in America, we'll not just be caring for our own souls, we'll be doing God's work here on Earth.

BENDING HISTORY
The Call to Serve
December 5, 2007

(Mt. Vernon, Iowa) Barack Obama delivered this campaign speech at Cornell College, taking as his theme the call to serve: *Decades from now ... when the words that we will speak in the next few years are long forgotten, I hope you remember this as a moment when your own story and the American story came together, and history bent once more in the direction of justice.*

Today, it's easy for us to get caught thinking that there are two different stories at work in our lives. There is the story of our day-to-day cares and responsibilities. And there is the story of what's happening in the wider world—a story viewed through headlines and websites, a destiny to be shaped by forces beyond our control.

I am here today to ask you to reject this notion, and to invite you to take hold of the future of your country. Because your own story and the American story are not separate—they are shared. And they will both be enriched if we stand up together, and answer a new call to service to meet the challenges of our new century.

I say this to you as someone whose presence on this stage is unlikely. My father came from thousands of miles away, in Kenya, and went back there soon after I was born. I spent a childhood adrift. I was raised in Hawaii and Indonesia. I lived with my single mom and with my grandparents from Kansas. Growing up, I wasn't always sure who I was, or where I was going.

Then, when I was about your age, I decided to become a community organizer. I wrote letters to every organization in the country that I could think of. And for a while I got no response. Finally, this small group of churches on the south side of Chicago wrote back and offered me a job to come help neighborhoods devastated by steel plant closings. My mother and grandparents wanted me to go to law school. My friends were applying to jobs on Wall Street. I didn't know a soul in Chicago, and the salary was about $12,000 a year, plus $2,000 to buy an old, beat-up car.

I still remember a conversation I had with an older man before I left. He looked and said, "Barack, I'll give you a bit of advice. Forget this community organizing business and do something that's gonna make you some money. You can't change the world, and people won't appreciate you trying. You've got a nice voice. What you should do is go into television broadcasting. I'm telling you, you've got a future."

Now, he may have had a point about the TV thing. And to tell you the truth, I didn't have a clear answer about what I was doing. I wanted to step into the currents of history and help people fight for their dreams, but didn't know what my role would be. I was inspired by what people ... did in the civil rights movement, but when I got to Chicago, there were no marches, no soaring speeches. In the shadow of an empty steel plant, there were just a lot of folks struggling. Day after day, I heard "no" a lot more than I heard "yes." I saw plenty of empty chairs in those meetings we put together.

But even as I discovered that you can't bend history to your will, I found that you could do your part to see that, in the words of Dr. King, it "bends toward justice." In church basements and around kitchen tables, block by block, we brought the community together, registered new voters, fought for new jobs, and helped people live lives with some measure of dignity.

Eventually, I realized I wasn't just helping other people. Through service, I found a community that embraced me—a church to belong to; citizenship that was meaningful, the direction I'd been seeking. Through service, I found that my own improbable story fit into a larger American story.

In America, each of us seeks our own dreams, but the sum of those dreams must be greater than ourselves. Because the America we inherited is the legacy of those who struggled, and those who served in so many ways, before us.

It's the legacy of a band of unlikely patriots who overthrew the tyranny of a King.

It's the legacy of abolitionists who stood up, and soldiers who fought for a more perfect union.

It's the legacy of those who started to teach in our schools and tend to the sick in our cities, who laid the rails and volunteered to uphold the law as America moved west.

It's the legacy of men who faced the Depression by putting on the uniform of the Civilian Conservation Corps, of women who worked on that Arsenal of Democracy and built the tanks and ships and bomber aircraft to fight fascism.

It's the legacy of those women's suffragists and freedom riders who stood up for justice, and young people who answered President Kennedy's call to go forth in a Peace Corps.

The sacrifices made by previous generations have never been easy. But America is a great nation precisely because Americans have been willing to stand up when it was hard, to serve on stages both great and small, to rise above moments of great challenge and terrible trial.

One of those moments took place on September 11, 2001. Whether you lived in Manhattan or here in Mount Vernon, you felt the pain and loss of that day not just as an individual, but as an American. That's why we lined up to give blood. That's why we held vigils and flew flags. That's why we rallied behind our President. We had a chance to step into the currents of history. We were ready to answer a new call for our country. But the call never came. Instead, we were asked to go shopping, and to prove our patriotism by supporting a war in Iraq that should never have been authorized, and never been waged.

We have lost precious time. Our nation is less secure and less respected in the world. Our energy dependence has risen, and so has the specter of climate change. More of our children have been left behind. Instead of a call to unity, we got a political strategy of division. The burden of service has fallen, more and more, on the brave men and women of our military who heroically serve tour after tour of duty in a war without end.

When I was thinking about whether or not to seek the presidency, there were some voices who counseled me to wait. You seem like a gifted young man, they said—why not wait around Washington a few more years? Or when I started talking about a politics of hope, some just rolled their eyes and echoed the words of that man from my younger days—you can't change the world, and people won't appreciate you trying.

Well I am running for President—right now—because I refuse to let this moment pass. The decisions we make today will shape the century that my daughters—and your children—grow up in. I have not served the cause of America for over two decades to stay on the sidelines at a time when that cause is being challenged at home and abroad. If we don't rise up to seize this moment, then we may not get another.

I have no doubt that in the face of impossible odds people who love their country can change it. But I hold no illusions that one man or woman can do this alone. That's why my campaign has called nearly 400,000 Americans to a common purpose. That's why I'm reaching out to Democrats, and also to Independents and Republicans. And that is why I won't just ask for your vote as a candidate; I will ask for your service and your active citizenship when I am President of the United States. This will not be a call issued in one speech or program; this will be a cause of my presidency.

First, we will create new opportunities for all Americans to serve, and to direct that service to our most pressing national challenges.

Americans have shown they want to step up. I see it everywhere I go—the brave young men and women who have signed up to defend our country, the volunteers fighting poverty in rural America and to rebuild New Orleans, students getting their colleges to divest to stop the genocide in Darfur, the thousands of young Americans who have flooded the applicant pool for Teach for America, retirees who are devoting their time to serve.

But we're not keeping pace with the demand of those who want to serve, and we're not leveraging that commitment to meet national challenges. FDR not only enlisted Americans to create employment; he targeted that service to build our infrastructure and conserve our environment. JFK not only called on a new generation; he made their service a bridge to the developing world, and a bright light of American values in the darkest days of the Cold War.

Today, AmeriCorps—our nation's network of local, state and national service programs—has 75,000 slots. As President, I will increase that to 250,000, and make that increased service a vehicle to meet national goals like providing health care and education, saving our planet and restoring our standing in the world, so that citizens see their efforts connected to a common purpose. People of all ages, stations, and skills will be asked to serve. Because, when it comes to the challenges we face, the American people are not the problem—they are the answer.

To help every American receive a world-class education, we will create a new Classroom Corps. We'll have college students, recent graduates, and retirees mentor young people; engineers and scientists will help make sure the next generation of innovators is educated here in America; civic, business, and faith leaders will develop new after-school programs for our kids.

To free ourselves from energy dependence and to confront climate change, we will create a new Energy Corps. We'll ask you to work on renewable energy projects, to teach folks about conservation, and to help clean up polluted areas. And we'll send talented American engineers and scientists abroad to help developing countries promote low-carbon energy development.

To restore America's standing, I will call on our greatest resource—not our bombs, guns, or dollars—I will call upon our people. We will grow the Foreign Service to renew our commitment to diplomacy. We will double the size of the Peace Corps by its 50th anniversary in 2011. And we'll reach out to other nations to engage their young people in similar programs, so that we work side by side to take on the common challenges that confront all humanity.

I will expand our military, while offering those who serve the promise that they will get the training, equipment, and care they deserve—and that they can trust we will never, ever, send them to fight in a misguided war. And we'll enlist veterans to help other veterans find jobs, to counsel vets who are confronting homelessness, mental health, and substance abuse problems, and to pitch in at VA hospitals and nursing homes.

Some of these programs will be full-time; some will be part-time opportunities for those who are working. And we'll expand and improve Senior Corps programs to attract new retirees with substantive service opportunities, so that service becomes a core part of active retirement.

And we'll use technology to connect people to service more extensively and effectively. We turn to websites like craigslist to find apartments and jobs. So we'll expand USA Freedom Corps to create an online network where Americans can browse opportunities to volunteer. You'll be able to search by category, time commitment, and skill sets; you'll be able to rate service opportunities, build service networks, and create your own service pages to track your hours and activities. This will empower more Americans to craft their own service agenda, and make their own change from the bottom up.

The second thing I'll do is invest in ideas that can help us meet our common challenges, because more often than not the next great social innovation won't be generated by the government.

The non-profit sector employs 1 in 12 Americans and 115 nonprofits are launched every day. Yet while the federal government invests $7 billion in research and development for the private sector, there is no similar effort to support non-profit innovation. Meanwhile, there are ideas across America—in our inner cities and small towns, from college graduates to folks making a career change—that could benefit millions of Americans if they're given the chance to grow.

As President, I will launch a new Social Investment Fund Network. It's time to get the grass roots, the foundations, the private sector, and the government at the table. We'll invest in ideas that work, leverage private sector dollars to encourage innovation, and expand successful programs to scale. Take a program like the Harlem Children's Zone, which helps thousands of kids in New York through after-school activities, mentoring, and family support. We need to make that model work in different cities around the country. And I'll start a new Social Entrepreneur Agency to make sure that small non-profits have the same kind of support that we give small businesses.

The third part of my plan will be integrating service into education, so that young Americans are called upon and prepared to be active citizens.

Just as we teach math and writing, arts and athletics, we need to teach young Americans to take citizenship seriously. Study after study shows that students who serve do better in school, are more likely to go to college, and more likely to maintain that service as adults. So when I'm President, I will set a goal for all American middle and high school students to perform 50 hours of service a year, and for all college students to perform 100 hours of service a year. This means that by the time you graduate college, you'll have done 17 weeks of service.

We'll reach this goal in several ways. At the middle and high school level, we'll make federal assistance conditional on school districts developing service programs, and give schools resources to offer new service opportunities. At the community level, we'll develop public-private partnerships so students can serve more outside the classroom.

For college students, I have proposed an annual American Opportunity Tax Credit of $4,000 to make tuition affordable. To receive this credit, we'll require 100 hours of public service. And we'll amend the Federal Work-Study program, so that nearly $250 million will help more than 200,000 college students work in part-time public service jobs each year.

And we will not leave out the nearly 2 million young Americans who are out of school and out of work. Instead, we'll use service to tighten their bond to the American family, and to put them on a pathway to success. We'll enlist them in a Green Job Corps, so that disadvantaged young people can find useful work and gain skills in a growing industry. And we'll expand the YouthBuild Program, which puts young Americans to work building affordable housing in America's poorest communities, giving them valuable skills and a chance to complete a high school education. Today, there are 8,000 YouthBuild slots—we'll expand that to 50,000.

Now I know what the cynics will say. I've heard from them all my life.

These are the voices that will tell you not just what you can't do but what you won't do. Americans won't come together—our allegiance doesn't go beyond our political party, region, or congregation. Young Americans won't serve their country—they're too selfish, or too lazy. This is the soft sell of the status quo, the voice that tells you to settle because settling isn't that bad.

Let me ask you to stop and consider this meeting that we're having. You go to the first school in the United States west of the Mississippi to grant women the same rights and privileges as men. You go to a school that resolved in 1870 that race would not be a factor in admission. These may be small changes on the vast canvas of history, but the America we live in is the sum total of that kind of courage, that spirit of progress. If it weren't for that kind of change, it wouldn't be possible for someone like me to stand here today to talk to you about the future of this country. You and I are at a place where somebody, at some point, decided that loving their community and their country meant doing something to change it.

Renewing that spirit starts with service. Make no mistake—our destiny as Americans is tied up with one another. If we are less respected in the world, then you will be less safe. If we keep paying dictators to fill up our gas tanks, then those oceans are going to rise. If we can't give our kids a world-class education, then our economy is going to fall behind.

.... It is time to recapture that sense of a common purpose—I am my brother's keeper, I am my sister's keeper. I'm tired of hearing about how America is on the wrong track—I want us to come together to put it on the right track. I'm tired of hearing about red America and blue America—I want to lead a United States of America. I'm tired of talking about what we can't do, or won't do, or won't even try—I want all of us to stand up and to start reaching for what is possible.

That's what history calls us to do. Because loving your country shouldn't just mean watching fireworks on the 4th of July; loving your country must mean accepting your responsibility to do your part to change it. And if you do stand up, I promise you that your life will be richer, and our country will be stronger.

We need your service, right now, in this moment—our moment—in history. I'm not going to tell you what your role should be; that's for you to discover. But I am going to ask you to play your part—ask you to stand up, ask you to put your foot firmly into the current of history. I am asking you to change history's course. And if I have the fortune to be your President, decades from now—when the memory of this or that policy has faded, and when the words that we will speak in the next few years are long forgotten—I hope you remember this as a moment when your own story and the American story came together, and history bent once more in the direction of justice.

ALWAYS HOPING, ALWAYS REACHING, ALWAYS STRIVING
The American Dream Speech
January 29, 2008

(El Dorado, Kansas) Barack Obama delivered this campaign speech at Butler Community College, taking as his theme the American dream: *It is a dream I share for your children and all of our children, and that is why it's American—always hoping, always reaching, always striving for that better day ahead.*

You know, we have been told for many years that we are becoming more divided as a nation.

We have been made to believe that differences of race and region—wealth and gender, party and religion have separated us into warring factions—into red states and blue states made up of individuals with opposing wants and needs, with conflicting hopes and dreams.

It is a vision of America that's been exploited and encouraged by pundits and politicians who need this division to score points and win elections. But it is a vision of America that I am running for President to fundamentally reject—not because of a blind optimism I hold, but because of a story I've lived.

It's a story that began here, in El Dorado, when a young man fell in love with a young woman who grew up down the road in Augusta. They came of age in the midst of the Depression, where he found odd jobs on small farms and oil rigs, always dodging the bank failures and foreclosures that were sweeping the nation.

They married just after war broke out in Europe, and he enlisted in Patton's army after the bombing of Pearl Harbor. She gave birth to their daughter on the base at Fort Leavenworth, and worked on a bomber assembly line when he left for war.

In a time of great uncertainty and anxiety, my grandparents held on to a simple dream—that they could raise my mother in a land of boundless opportunity, that their generation's struggle and sacrifice could give her the freedom to be what she wanted to be, to live how she wanted to live.

I am standing here today because that dream was realized—because my grandfather got the chance to go to school on the GI Bill, buy a house through the Federal Housing Authority, and move his family west, all the way to Hawaii, where my mother would go to college and one day fall in love with a young student from Kenya.

I am here because that dream made my parents' love possible, even then, because it meant that after my father left, when my mother struggled as a single parent, and even turned to food stamps for a time, she was still able to send my sister and me to the best schools in the country.

And I'm here because years later, when I found my own love in a place far away called Chicago, she told me of a similar dream. Michelle grew up in a working-class family on the South Side during the 1960s. Her father had been diagnosed with multiple sclerosis at just thirty years old. And yet, every day of his life, even when he had to rely on a walker to get him there, Fraser Robinson went to work at the local water filtration plant while his wife stayed home with the children. And on that single salary, he was able to send Michelle and her brother to Princeton.

Our family's story is one that spans miles and generations, races and realities. It's the story of farmers and soldiers, city workers and single moms. It takes place in small towns and good schools, in Kansas and Kenya, on the shores of Hawaii and the streets of Chicago. It's a varied and unlikely journey, but one that's held together by the same simple dream.

And that is why it's American.

That's why I can stand here and talk about how this country is more than a collection of red states and blue states—because my story could only happen in the United States.

That's why I believe that we are not as divided as our politics suggests, that the dream we share is more powerful than the differences we have, because I am living proof of that ideal.

And that is what I have seen all across this country over the course of this campaign.

I've seen crumbling schools in South Carolina that are stealing the future of black children and white children.

I've been told of the injustice in the growing divide between Main Street and Wall Street by the lowest-paid workers and the wealthiest billionaires.

I've met autoworkers in Iowa and teachers in New Hampshire and dishwashers in Nevada who are all fighting the same fight for better wages and good benefits and a retirement they can count on.

And I've talked to young people and old people; Democrats, Independents, and Republicans who love their country, support their troops, and believe it is time to bring them home from Iraq.

We are not as divided as our politics suggest. Yes, we disagree. Yes, we have interests and ideologies that don't always align. Yes, we have real differences.

But the biggest divide in America today is not between its people. It is between its people and their leaders in Washington, DC. That is where our collective dream has been deferred.... And that's where politicians would rather demonize each other to score points than come together to solve our common challenges.

That is where the real division lies—in a politics that echoes through the media and seeps into our culture—the kind that seeks to drive us apart and put up walls where none exist.

It's the politics that tells us that those who differ from us on a few things are different from us on all things, that our problems are the fault of those who don't think like us or look like us or come from where we do. The welfare queen is taking our tax money. The immigrant is taking our jobs. The gay person must be immoral, and the believer must be intolerant.

Well, we are here to say that this is not the America we believe in and this is not the politics we have to accept anymore. Not this time. Not now.

This will not be easy. Because the change we seek will not just come from overcoming the ingrained and destructive habits of Washington; it will require overcoming our own fears and our own doubts. It will require each of us to do our part in closing the moral deficit—the empathy deficit—that exists in this nation. It will take standing in one another's shoes and remembering that we are our brother's keeper; we are our sister's keeper.

This will not be easy, but America's story tells me it's possible. My story tells me it's possible. What began here in Kansas all those years ago tells me it's possible.

Because as we face another time of anxiety and uncertainty—a time where foreclosures sweep the nation and families struggle to stay afloat; where loved ones leave for war and parents wonder what kind of world their children will inherit—I believe that this nation can rally around the simple dream that my grandparents held on to even in the darkest of days.

It's a dream that we can find a job with wages that support a family. That we can have health care that's affordable for when we get sick. That we can retire with dignity and security. And that we can provide our children with education and opportunity—so that they can be what they want to be and live how they want to live. They are the common dreams that can finally unite a nation around a common purpose.

There are those who will continue to tell us we cannot do this. That we cannot come together. That the divisions in our politics run too deep. That we are offering the American people false hopes.

But here's what I know.

I know that when I hear people say that we can't come together to lift up working families who are struggling in this economy, I think back to the streets of Chicago, where I began my career as a community organizer twenty-five years ago. In the shadow of a closed steel mill, we brought white people and black people and Latinos together to provide job training to the jobless and after school programs for children. Block by block, we restored hope and opportunity to those neighborhoods, and I can believe we can do the same thing for the working families of America.

Right now, there's an economic stimulus package moving through Congress that will provide a boost to the economy and to working families.... I hope that when it's final, it will also provide relief to seniors and extend unemployment insurance to those who've lost their jobs.

But we need to do even more to restore fairness and balance to our economy. Last night, we heard the President say that he wanted to make his tax cuts for the wealthiest Americans permanent—again…. It's time to give tax relief to the middle-class families who need it right now.

…. And when I hear that some of our kids just can't learn; that we can't do anything about crumbling schools and rising tuition, I think back to the chances that somebody, somewhere gave my family. The ticket my father got to come study in America. The opportunity my mother had to put herself through graduate school. The chance I had to go to the best schools in the country, even though we didn't have much.

It is time to give every child in America that kind of chance, no matter what they look like or where they come from….

This election is our chance—our moment—to restore the simple dream of those who came before us for another generation of Americans. But only if we can come together like previous generations did and close that divide between a people and its leaders in Washington.

Because in the end, the choice in this election is not between regions or religions or genders. It's not about rich versus poor, young versus old; and it is not about black versus white.

It's about the past versus the future. It's about whether we settle for the same divisions and distractions and drama that passes for politics today, or whether we reach for a politics of common sense and innovation, of shared sacrifice and shared prosperity.

In the face of war and depression, through great struggle and tremendous sacrifice—that is the future that my grandparents' generation forged for their children. It is why that little girl who was born at Fort Leavenworth could dream as big as the Kansas sky. And it is why I stand before you today—because there are two little girls I tuck in at night who deserve a world in which they can dream those same big dreams, in which they can have the same chances as any other child living any other place. It is a dream I share for your children and all of our children, and that is why it's American—always hoping, always reaching, always striving for that better day ahead. I hope you'll join me on that journey, and I thank you for welcoming me back to the place my family called home.

A MORE PERFECT UNION
The Race Speech
March 18, 2008

(Philadelphia, Pennsylvania) Barack Obama delivered this campaign speech at the Constitution Center, taking as his theme healing racial wounds: *I have asserted a firm conviction—a conviction rooted in my faith in God and my faith in the American people—that working together we can move beyond some of our old racial wounds, and that in fact we have no choice if we are to continue on the path of a more perfect union.*

"We the people, in order to form a more perfect union."

Two hundred and twenty-one years ago, in a hall that still stands across the street, a group of men gathered and, with these simple words, launched America's improbable experiment in democracy. Farmers and scholars; statesmen and patriots who had traveled across an ocean to escape tyranny and persecution finally made real their declaration of independence at a Philadelphia convention that lasted through the spring of 1787.

The document they produced was eventually signed but ultimately unfinished. It was stained by this nation's original sin of slavery, a question that divided the colonies and brought the convention to a stalemate until the founders chose to allow the slave trade to continue for at least twenty more years, and to leave any final resolution to future generations.

Of course, the answer to the slavery question was already embedded within our Constitution—a Constitution that had at is very core the ideal of equal citizenship under the law, a Constitution that promised its people liberty, and justice, and a union that could be and should be perfected over time.

And yet words on a parchment would not be enough to deliver slaves from bondage, or provide men and women of every color and creed their full rights and obligations as citizens of the United States. What would be needed were Americans in successive generations who were willing to do their part—through protests and struggle, on the streets and in the courts, through a civil war and civil disobedience and always at great risk—to narrow that gap between the promise of our ideals and the reality of their time.

This was one of the tasks we set forth at the beginning of this campaign—to continue the long march of those who came before us, a march for a more just, more equal, more free, more caring, and more prosperous America. I chose to run for the presidency at this moment in history because I believe deeply that we cannot solve the challenges of our time unless we solve them together—unless we perfect our union by understanding that we may have different stories, but we hold common hopes, that we may not look the same and we may not have come from the same place, but we all want to move in the same direction—towards a better future for our children and our grandchildren.

This belief comes from my unyielding faith in the decency and generosity of the American people. But it also comes from my own American story.

I am the son of a black man from Kenya and a white woman from Kansas. I was raised with the help of a white grandfather who survived a Depression to serve in Patton's Army during World War II and a white grandmother who worked on a bomber assembly line at Fort Leavenworth while he was overseas. I've gone to some of the best schools in America and lived in one of the world's poorest nations. I am married to a black American who carries within her the blood of slaves and slaveowners—an inheritance we pass on to our two precious daughters. I have brothers, sisters, nieces, nephews, uncles, and cousins, of every race and every hue, scattered across three continents and, for as long as I live, I will never forget that in no other country on Earth is my story even possible.

It's a story that hasn't made me the most conventional candidate. But it is a story that has seared into my genetic makeup the idea that this nation is more than the sum of its parts—that out of many, we are truly one.

Throughout the first year of this campaign, against all predictions to the contrary, we saw how hungry the American people were for this message of unity. Despite the temptation to view my candidacy through a purely racial lens, we won commanding victories in states with some of the whitest populations in the country. In South Carolina, where the Confederate Flag still flies, we built a powerful coalition of African-Americans and white Americans.

This is not to say that race has not been an issue in the campaign. At various stages in the campaign, some commentators have deemed me either "too black" or "not black enough." We saw racial tensions bubble to the surface during the week before the South Carolina primary. The press has scoured every exit poll for the latest evidence of racial polarization, not just in terms of white and black, but black and brown as well.

And yet it has only been in the last couple of weeks that the discussion of race in this campaign has taken a particularly divisive turn.

On one end of the spectrum, we've heard the implication that my candidacy is somehow an exercise in affirmative action, that it's based solely on the desire of wide-eyed liberals to purchase racial reconciliation on the cheap. On the other end, we've heard my former pastor, Reverend Jeremiah Wright, use incendiary language to express views that have the potential not only to widen the racial divide, but views that denigrate both the greatness and the goodness of our nation, that rightly offend white and black alike.

I have already condemned, in unequivocal terms, the statements of Reverend Wright that have caused such controversy. For some, nagging questions remain. Did I know him to be an occasionally fierce critic of American domestic and foreign policy? Of course. Did I ever hear him make remarks that could be considered controversial while I sat in church? Yes. Did I strongly disagree with many of his political views? Absolutely—just as I'm sure many of you have heard remarks from your pastors, priests, or rabbis with which you strongly disagreed.

But the remarks that have caused this recent firestorm weren't simply controversial. They weren't simply a religious leader's effort to speak out against perceived injustice. Instead, they expressed a profoundly distorted view of this country—a view that sees white racism as endemic, and that elevates what is wrong with America above all that we know is right with America—a view that sees the conflicts in the Middle East as rooted primarily in the actions of stalwart allies like Israel, instead of emanating from the perverse and hateful ideologies of radical Islam.

As such, Reverend Wright's comments were not only wrong but divisive, divisive at a time when we need unity, racially charged at a time when we need to come together to solve a set of monumental problems—two wars, a terrorist threat, a falling economy, a chronic health care crisis, and potentially devastating climate change—problems that are neither black nor white nor Latino nor Asian, but rather problems that confront us all.

Given my background, my politics, and my professed values and ideals, there will no doubt be those for whom my statements of condemnation are not enough. Why associate myself with Reverend Wright in the first place, they may ask? Why not join another church? And I confess that if all that I knew of Reverend Wright were the snippets of those sermons that have run in an endless loop on the television and YouTube, or if Trinity United Church of Christ conformed to the caricatures being peddled by some commentators, there is no doubt that I would react in much the same way

But the truth is, that isn't all that I know of the man. The man I met more than twenty years ago is a man who helped introduce me to my Christian faith, a man who spoke to me about our obligations to love one another, to care for the sick and lift up the poor. He is a man who served his country as a U.S. Marine, who has studied and lectured at some of the finest universities and seminaries in the country, and who for over thirty years led a church that serves the community by doing God's work here on Earth—by housing the homeless, ministering to the needy, providing day care services and scholarships and prison ministries, and reaching out to those suffering from HIV/AIDS.

In my first book, *Dreams From My Father*, I described the experience of my first service at Trinity:

> "People began to shout, to rise from their seats and clap and cry out, a forceful wind carrying the reverend's voice up into the rafters.... And in that single note—hope!—I heard something else; at the foot of that cross, inside the thousands of churches across the city, I imagined the stories of ordinary black people merging with the stories of David and Goliath, Moses and Pharaoh, the Christians in

the lion's den, Ezekiel's field of dry bones. Those stories—of survival, and freedom, and hope—became our story, my story; the blood that had spilled was our blood, the tears our tears; until this black church, on this bright day, seemed once more a vessel carrying the story of a people into future generations and into a larger world. Our trials and triumphs became at once unique and universal, black and more than black; in chronicling our journey, the stories and songs gave us a means to reclaim memories that we didn't need to feel shame about … memories that all people might study and cherish—and with which we could start to rebuild."

That has been my experience at Trinity. Like other predominantly black churches across the country, Trinity embodies the black community in its entirety—the doctor and the welfare mom, the model student and the former gang-banger. Like other black churches, Trinity's services are full of raucous laughter and sometimes bawdy humor. They are full of dancing, clapping, screaming, and shouting that may seem jarring to the untrained ear. The church contains in full the kindness and cruelty, the fierce intelligence and the shocking ignorance, the struggles and successes, the love and yes, the bitterness and bias that make up the black experience in America.

And this helps explain, perhaps, my relationship with Reverend Wright. As imperfect as he may be, he has been like family to me. He strengthened my faith, officiated my wedding, and baptized my children. Not once in my conversations with him have I heard him talk about any ethnic group in derogatory terms, or treat whites with whom he interacted with anything but courtesy and respect. He contains within him the contradictions—the good and the bad—of the community that he has served diligently for so many years.

I can no more disown him than I can disown the black community. I can no more disown him than I can my white grandmother—a woman who helped raise me, a woman who sacrificed again and again for me, a woman who loves me as much as she loves anything in this world, but a woman who once confessed her fear of black men who passed by her on the street, and who on more than one occasion has uttered racial or ethnic stereotypes that made me cringe.

These people are a part of me. And they are a part of America, this country that I love.

Some will see this as an attempt to justify or excuse comments that are simply inexcusable. I can assure you it is not. I suppose the politically safe thing would be to move on from this episode and just hope that it fades into the woodwork. We can dismiss Reverend Wright as a crank or a demagogue, just as some have dismissed Geraldine Ferraro, in the aftermath of her recent statements, as harboring some deep-seated racial bias.

But race is an issue that I believe this nation cannot afford to ignore right now. We would be making the same mistake that Reverend Wright made in his offending sermons about America—to simplify and stereotype and amplify the negative to the point that it distorts reality.

The fact is that the comments that have been made and the issues that have surfaced over the last few weeks reflect the complexities of race in this country that we've never really worked through—a part of our union that we have yet to perfect. And if we walk away now, if we simply retreat into our respective corners, we will never be able to come together and solve challenges like health care, or education, or the need to find good jobs for every American.

Understanding this reality requires a reminder of how we arrived at this point. As William Faulkner once wrote,

"The past isn't dead and buried. In fact, it isn't even past."

We do not need to recite here the history of racial injustice in this country. But we do need to remind ourselves that so many of the disparities that exist in the African-American community today can be directly traced to inequalities passed on from an earlier generation that suffered under the brutal legacy of slavery and Jim Crow.

Segregated schools were, and are, inferior schools; we still haven't fixed them, fifty years after *Brown v. Board of Education*, and the inferior education they provided, then and now, helps explain the pervasive achievement gap between today's black and white students.

Legalized discrimination—where blacks were prevented, often through violence, from owning property, or loans were not granted to African-American business owners, or black homeowners could not access FHA mortgages, or blacks were excluded from unions, or the police force, or fire departments—meant that black families could not amass any meaningful wealth to bequeath to future generations. That history helps explain the wealth and income gap between black and white, and the concentrated pockets of poverty that persist in so many of today's urban and rural communities.

A lack of economic opportunity among black men, and the shame and frustration that came from not being able to provide for one's family, contributed to the erosion of black families—a problem that welfare policies for many years may have worsened. And the lack of basic services in so many urban black neighborhoods—parks for kids to play in, police walking the beat, regular garbage pick-up and building code enforcement—all helped create a cycle of violence, blight, and neglect that continue to haunt us.

This is the reality in which Reverend Wright and other African-Americans of his generation grew up. They came of age in the late fifties and early sixties, a time when segregation was still the law of the land and opportunity was systematically constricted. What's remarkable is not how many failed in the face of discrimination, but rather how many men and women overcame the odds, how many were able to make a way out of no way for those like me who would come after them.

But for all those who scratched and clawed their way to get a piece of the American Dream, there were many who didn't make it—those who were ultimately defeated, in one way or another, by discrimination. That legacy of defeat was passed on to future generations—those young men and increasingly young women who we see standing on street corners or languishing in our prisons, without hope or prospects for the future. Even for those blacks who did make it, questions of race, and racism, continue to define their world view in fundamental ways. For the men and women of Reverend Wright's generation, the memories of humiliation and doubt and fear have not gone away; nor has the anger and the bitterness of those years. That anger may not get expressed in public, in front of white co-workers or white friends. But it does find voice in the barbershop or around the kitchen table. At times, that anger is exploited by politicians, to gin up votes along racial lines, or to make up for a politician's own failings.

And occasionally it finds voice in the church on Sunday morning, in the pulpit and in the pews. The fact that so many people are surprised to hear that anger in some of Reverend Wright's sermons simply reminds us of the old truism that the most segregated hour in American life occurs on Sunday morning. That anger is not always productive; indeed, all too often it distracts attention from solving real problems; it keeps us from squarely facing our own complicity in our condition, and prevents the African-American community from forging the alliances it needs to bring about real change. But the anger is real; it is powerful; and to simply wish it away, to condemn it without understanding its roots, only serves to widen the chasm of misunderstanding that exists between the races.

In fact, a similar anger exists within segments of the white community. Most working- and middle-class white Americans don't feel that they have been particularly privileged by their race. Their experience is the immigrant experience—as far as they're concerned, no one's handed them anything, they've built it from scratch. They've worked hard all their lives, many times only to see their jobs shipped overseas or their pension dumped after a lifetime of labor. They are anxious about their futures, and feel their dreams slipping away; in an era of stagnant wages and global competition, opportunity comes to be seen as a zero sum game, in which your dreams come at my expense. So when they are told to bus their children to a school across town, when they hear that an African-American is getting an advantage in landing a good job or a spot in a good college because of an injustice that they themselves never committed, when they're told that their fears about crime in urban neighborhoods are somehow prejudiced, resentment builds over time.

Like the anger within the black community, these resentments aren't always expressed in polite company. But they have helped shape the political landscape for at least a generation. Anger over welfare and affirmative action helped forge the Reagan Coalition. Politicians routinely exploited fears of crime for their own electoral ends. Talk show hosts and conservative commentators built entire careers unmasking bogus claims of racism while dismissing legitimate discussions of racial injustice and inequality as mere political correctness or reverse racism.

Just as black anger often proved counterproductive, so have these white resentments distracted attention from the real culprits of the middle class squeeze—a corporate culture rife with inside dealing, questionable accounting practices, and short-term greed, a Washington dominated by lobbyists and special interests, economic policies that favor the few over the many. And yet to wish away the resentments of white Americans—to label them as misguided or even racist, without recognizing they are grounded in legitimate concerns—this too widens the racial divide, and blocks the path to understanding.

This is where we are right now. It's a racial stalemate we've been stuck in for years. Contrary to the claims of some of my critics, black and white, I have never been so naïve as to believe that we can get beyond our racial divisions in a single election cycle, or with a single candidacy, particularly a candidacy as imperfect as my own. But I have asserted a firm conviction—a conviction rooted in my faith in God and my faith in the American people— that working together we can move beyond some of our old racial wounds, and that in fact we have no choice if we are to continue on the path of a more perfect union.

For the African-American community, that path means embracing the burdens of our past without becoming victims of our past. It means continuing to insist on a full measure of justice in every aspect of American life. But it also means binding our particular grievances—for better health care, and better schools, and better jobs—to the larger aspirations of all Americans—the white woman struggling to break the glass ceiling, the white man who's been laid off, the immigrant trying to feed his family. And it means taking full responsibility for own lives—by demanding more from our fathers, and spending more time with our children, and reading to them, and teaching them that, while they may face challenges and discrimination in their own lives, they must never succumb to despair or cynicism; they must always believe that they can write their own destiny.

Ironically, this quintessentially American—and yes, conservative—notion of self-help found frequent expression in Reverend Wright's sermons. But what my former pastor too often failed to understand is that embarking on a program of self-help also requires a belief that society can change. The profound mistake of Reverend Wright's sermons is not that he spoke about racism in our society. It's that he spoke as if our society was static, as if no progress has been made, as if this country—a country that has made it possible for one of his own members to run for the highest office in the land and build a coalition of white and black, Latino and Asian, rich and poor, young and old—is still irrevocably bound to a tragic past. But what we know—what we have seen—is that America can change. That is true genius of this nation. What we have already achieved gives us hope— the audacity to hope—for what we can and must achieve tomorrow.

In the white community, the path to a more perfect union means acknowledging that what ails the African-American community does not just exist in the minds of black people, that the legacy of discrimination, and current incidents of discrimination (while less overt than in the past), are real and must be addressed. Not just with words, but with deeds—by investing in our schools and our communities, by enforcing our civil rights laws and ensuring fairness in our criminal justice system, by providing this generation with ladders of opportunity that were unavailable for previous generations. It requires all Americans to realize that your dreams do not have to come at the expense of my dreams, that investing in the health, welfare, and education of black and brown and white children will ultimately help all of America prosper.

In the end, then, what is called for is nothing more, and nothing less, than what all the world's great religions demand—that we do unto others as we would have them do unto us. Let us be our brother's keeper, Scripture tells us. Let us be our sister's keeper. Let us find that common stake we all have in one another, and let our politics reflect that spirit as well.

For we have a choice in this country. We can accept a politics that breeds division, and conflict, and cynicism. We can tackle race only as spectacle—as we did in the OJ trial— or in the wake of tragedy—as we did in the aftermath of Katrina—or as fodder for the nightly news. We can play Reverend Wright's sermons on every channel every day and talk about them from now until the election, and make the only question in this campaign whether or not the American people think that I somehow believe or sympathize with his most offensive words. We can pounce on some gaffe by a Hillary supporter as evidence that she's playing the race card, or we can speculate on whether white men will all flock to John McCain in the general election regardless of his policies.

We can do that.

But if we do, I can tell you that in the next election we'll be talking about some other distraction. And then another one. And then another one. And nothing will change.

That is one option. Or, at this moment, in this election, we can come together and say, "Not this time." This time we want to talk about the crumbling schools that are stealing the future of black children and white children and Asian children and Hispanic children and Native American children. This time we want to reject the cynicism that tells us that these kids can't learn, that those kids who don't look like us are somebody else's problem. The children of America are not those kids—they are our kids—and we will not let them fall behind in a 21st century economy. Not this time.

This time we want to talk about how the lines in the emergency room are filled with whites and blacks and Hispanics who do not have health care; who don't have the power on their own to overcome the special interests in Washington, but who can take them on if we do it together.

This time we want to talk about the shuttered mills that once provided a decent life for men and women of every race, and the homes for sale that once belonged to Americans from every religion, every region, every walk of life. This time we want to talk about the fact that the real problem is not that someone who doesn't look like you might take your job—it's that the corporation you work for will ship it overseas for nothing more than a profit.

This time we want to talk about the men and women of every color and creed who serve together, and fight together, and bleed together under the same proud flag. We want to talk about how to bring them home from a war that never should've been authorized and never should've been waged, and we want to talk about how we'll show our patriotism by caring for them, and their families, and giving them the benefits they have earned.

I would not be running for President if I didn't believe with all my heart that this is what the vast majority of Americans want for this country. This union may never be perfect, but generation after generation has shown that it can always be perfected. And today, whenever I find myself feeling doubtful or cynical about this possibility, what gives me the most hope is the next generation—the young people whose attitudes and beliefs and openness to change have already made history in this election.

There is one story in particularly that I'd like to leave you with today—a story I told when I had the great honor of speaking on Dr. King's birthday at his home church, Ebenezer Baptist, in Atlanta.

There is a young, twenty-three-year-old white woman named Ashley Baia who organized for our campaign in Florence, South Carolina. She had been working to organize a mostly African-American community since the beginning of this campaign, and one day she was at a roundtable discussion where everyone went around telling their story and why they were there.

And Ashley said that when she was nine years old, her mother got cancer. And because she had to miss days of work, she was let go and lost her health care. They had to file for bankruptcy, and that's when Ashley decided that she had to do something to help her mom.

She knew that food was one of their most expensive costs, and so Ashley convinced her mother that what she really liked and really wanted to eat more than anything else was mustard and relish sandwiches. Because that was the cheapest way to eat.

She did this for a year until her mom got better, and she told everyone at the roundtable that the reason she joined our campaign was so that she could help the millions of other children in the country who want and need to help their parents too.

Now Ashley might have made a different choice. Perhaps somebody told her along the way that the source of her mother's problems were blacks who were on welfare and too lazy to work, or Hispanics who were coming into the country illegally. But she didn't. She sought out allies in her fight against injustice.

Anyway, Ashley finishes her story and then goes around the room and asks everyone else why they're supporting the campaign. They all have different stories and reasons. Many bring up a specific issue. And finally they come to this elderly black man who's been sitting there quietly the entire time. And Ashley asks him why he's there. And he does not bring up a specific issue. He does not say health care or the economy. He does not say education or the war. He does not say that he was there because of Barack Obama. He simply says to everyone in the room, "I am here because of Ashley."

"I'm here because of Ashley." By itself, that single moment of recognition between that young white girl and that old black man is not enough. It is not enough to give health care to the sick, or jobs to the jobless, or education to our children.

But it is where we start. It is where our union grows stronger. And as so many generations have come to realize, over the course of the two hundred and twenty-one years since a band of patriots signed that document in Philadelphia, that is where the perfection begins.

THE AMERICAN SPIRIT,
THE AMERICAN PROMISE
Acceptance Of The Democratic Nomination
August 28, 2008

(Denver, Colorado) Barack Obama delivered this speech, accepting the nomination of the Democratic Party as their candidate in the race for President: *It is that American spirit—that American promise—that pushes us forward even when the path is uncertain, that binds us together in spite of our differences, that makes us fix our eye not on what is seen, but what is unseen, that better place around the bend.*

Four years ago, I stood before you and told you my story—of the brief union between a young man from Kenya and a young woman from Kansas who weren't well-off or well-known, but shared a belief that, in America, their son could achieve whatever he put his mind to.

It is that promise that has always set this country apart—that through hard work and sacrifice, each of us can pursue our individual dreams but still come together as one American family, to ensure that the next generation can pursue their dreams as well.

That's why I stand here tonight. Because for two hundred and thirty-two years, at each moment when that promise was in jeopardy, ordinary men and women—students and soldiers, farmers and teachers, nurses and janitors—found the courage to keep it alive.

We meet at one of those defining moments—a moment when our nation is at war, our economy is in turmoil, and the American promise has been threatened once more.

Tonight, more Americans are out of work and more are working harder for less. More of you have lost your homes and even more are watching your home values plummet. More of you have cars you can't afford to drive, credit card bills you can't afford to pay, and tuition that's beyond your reach. These challenges are not all of government's making. But the failure to respond is a direct result of a broken politics in Washington and the failed policies of George W. Bush.

America, we are better than these last eight years. We are a better country than this.

This country is more decent than one where a woman in Ohio, on the brink of retirement, finds herself one illness away from disaster after a lifetime of hard work.

This country is more generous than one where a man in Indiana has to pack up the equipment he's worked on for twenty years and watch it shipped off to China, and then chokes up as he explains how he felt like a failure when he went home to tell his family the news.

We are more compassionate than a government that lets veterans sleep on our streets and families slide into poverty, that sits on its hands while a major American city drowns before our eyes.

Tonight, I say to the American people, to Democrats and Republicans and Independents across this great land—enough! This moment—this election—is our chance to keep, in the 21st century, the American promise alive. Because next week, in Minnesota, the same party that brought you two terms of George Bush and Dick Cheney will ask this country for a third. And we are here because we love this country too much to let the next four years look like the last eight. On November 4th, we must stand up and say, "Eight is enough."

.... It's time for us to change America. You see, we Democrats have a very different measure of what constitutes progress in this country. We measure progress by how many people can find a job that pays the mortgage, whether you can put a little extra money away at the end of each month so you can someday watch your child receive her college diploma. We measure progress in the 23 million new jobs that were created when Bill Clinton was President—when the average American family saw its income go up $7,500 instead of down $2,000 like it has under George Bush.

We measure the strength of our economy not by the number of billionaires we have or the profits of the Fortune 500, but by whether someone with a good idea can take a risk and start a new business, or whether the waitress who lives on tips can take a day off to look after a sick kid without losing her job—an economy that honors the dignity of work.

The fundamentals we use to measure economic strength are whether we are living up to that fundamental promise that has made this country great—a promise that is the only reason I am standing here tonight.

Because in the faces of those young veterans who come back from Iraq and Afghanistan, I see my grandfather, who signed up after Pearl Harbor, marched in Patton's Army, and was rewarded by a grateful nation with the chance to go to college on the GI Bill.

In the face of that young student who sleeps just three hours before working the night shift, I think about my mom, who raised my sister and me on her own while she worked and earned her degree; who once turned to food stamps but was still able to send us to the best schools in the country with the help of student loans and scholarships.

When I listen to another worker tell me that his factory has shut down, I remember all those men and women on the South Side of Chicago who I stood by and fought for two decades ago after the local steel plant closed.

And when I hear a woman talk about the difficulties of starting her own business, I think about my grandmother, who worked her way up from the secretarial pool to middle-management, despite years of being passed over for promotions because she was a woman. She's the one who taught me about hard work. She's the one who put off buying a new car or a new dress for herself so that I could have a better life. She poured everything she had into me. And although she can no longer travel, I know that she's watching tonight, and that tonight is her night as well.

.... These are my heroes. Theirs are the stories that shaped me. And it is on their behalf that I intend to win this election and keep our promise alive as President of the United States.

What is that promise?

It's a promise that says each of us has the freedom to make of our own lives what we will, but that we also have the obligation to treat each other with dignity and respect.

It's a promise that says the market should reward drive and innovation and generate growth, but that businesses should live up to their responsibilities to create American jobs, look out for American workers, and play by the rules of the road.

Ours is a promise that says government cannot solve all our problems, but what it should do is that which we cannot do for ourselves—protect us from harm and provide every child a decent education, keep our water clean and our toys safe, invest in new schools and new roads and new science and technology.

Our government should work for us, not against us. It should help us, not hurt us. It should ensure opportunity not just for those with the most money and influence, but for every American who's willing to work.

That's the promise of America—the idea that we are responsible for ourselves, but that we also rise or fall as one nation—the fundamental belief that I am my brother's keeper; I am my sister's keeper.

That's the promise we need to keep. That's the change we need right now. So let me spell out exactly what that change would mean if I am President.

Change means a tax code that doesn't reward the lobbyists who wrote it, but the American workers and small businesses who deserve it.... I will stop giving tax breaks to corporations that ship jobs overseas, and I will start giving them to companies that create good jobs right here in America. I will eliminate capital gains taxes for the small businesses and the start-ups that will create the high-wage, high-tech jobs of tomorrow.

I will cut taxes—cut taxes—for 95% of all working families. Because in an economy like this, the last thing we should do is raise taxes on the middle class.

And for the sake of our economy, our security, and the future of our planet, I will set a clear goal as President—in ten years, we will finally end our dependence on oil from the Middle East. Washington's been talking about our oil addiction for the last thirty years.... Now is the time to end this addiction, and to understand that drilling is a stop-gap measure, not a long-term solution. Not even close.

As President, I will tap our natural gas reserves, invest in clean coal technology, and find ways to safely harness nuclear power. I'll help our auto companies re-tool, so that the fuel-efficient cars of the future are built right here in America. I'll make it easier for the American people to afford these new cars. And I'll invest 150 billion dollars over the next decade in affordable, renewable sources of energy—wind power and solar power and the next generation of biofuels—an investment that will lead to new industries and five million new jobs that pay well and can't ever be outsourced.

America, now is not the time for small plans.

Now is the time to finally meet our moral obligation to provide every child a world-class education, because it will take nothing less to compete in the global economy. Michelle and I are only here tonight because we were given a chance at an education. And I will not settle for an America where some kids don't have that chance. I'll invest in early childhood education. I'll recruit an army of new teachers, and pay them higher salaries and give them more support. And in exchange, I'll ask for higher standards and more accountability. And we will keep our promise to every young American—if you commit to serving your community or your country, we will make sure you can afford a college education.

Now is the time to finally keep the promise of affordable, accessible health care for every single American. If you have health care, my plan will lower your premiums. If you don't, you'll be able to get the same kind of coverage that members of Congress give themselves. And as someone who watched my mother argue with insurance companies while she lay in bed dying of cancer, I will make certain those companies stop discriminating against those who are sick and need care the most.

Now is the time to help families with paid sick days and better family leave, because nobody in America should have to choose between keeping their jobs and caring for a sick child or ailing parent.

Now is the time to change our bankruptcy laws, so that your pensions are protected ahead of CEO bonuses, and the time to protect Social Security for future generations.

And now is the time to keep the promise of equal pay for an equal day's work, because I want my daughters to have exactly the same opportunities as your sons.

Now, many of these plans will cost money, which is why I've laid out how I'll pay for every dime—by closing corporate loopholes and tax havens that don't help America grow. But I will also go through the federal budget, line by line, eliminating programs that no longer work and making the ones we do need work better and cost less—because we cannot meet 21st century challenges with a 20th century bureaucracy.

And Democrats, we must also admit that fulfilling America's promise will require more than just money. It will require a renewed sense of responsibility from each of us to recover what John F. Kennedy called our "intellectual and moral strength." Yes, government must lead on energy independence, but each of us must do our part to make our homes and businesses more efficient. Yes, we must provide more ladders to success for young men who fall into lives of crime and despair. But we must also admit that programs alone can't replace parents, that government can't turn off the television and make a child do her homework, that fathers must take more responsibility for providing the love and guidance their children need.

Individual responsibility and mutual responsibility—that's the essence of America's promise.

And just as we keep our keep our promise to the next generation here at home, so must we keep America's promise abroad…. We need a President who can face the threats of the future, not keep grasping at the ideas of the past….

We are the party of Roosevelt. We are the party of Kennedy. So don't tell me that Democrats won't defend this country. Don't tell me that Democrats won't keep us safe. The Bush-McCain foreign policy has squandered the legacy that generations of Americans—Democrats and Republicans—have built, and we are here to restore that legacy.

As Commander-in-Chief, I will never hesitate to defend this nation, but I will only send our troops into harm's way with a clear mission and a sacred commitment to give them the equipment they need in battle and the care and benefits they deserve when they come home.

I will end this war in Iraq responsibly, and finish the fight against al Qaeda and the Taliban in Afghanistan. I will rebuild our military to meet future conflicts. But I will also renew the tough, direct diplomacy that can prevent Iran from obtaining nuclear weapons and curb Russian aggression. I will build new partnerships to defeat the threats of the 21st century—terrorism and nuclear proliferation, poverty and genocide, climate change and disease. And I will restore our moral standing, so that America is once again that last, best hope for all who are called to the cause of freedom, who long for lives of peace, and who yearn for a better future.

These are the policies I will pursue....

[One] of the things that we have to change in our politics is the idea that people cannot disagree without challenging each other's character and patriotism. The times are too serious, the stakes are too high for this same partisan playbook. So let us agree that patriotism has no party. I love this country, and so do you, and so does John McCain. The men and women who serve in our battlefields may be Democrats and Republicans and Independents, but they have fought together and bled together and some died together under the same proud flag. They have not served a Red America or a Blue America—they have served the United States of America.... We all put our country first.

America, our work will not be easy. The challenges we face require tough choices, and Democrats as well as Republicans will need to cast off the worn-out ideas and politics of the past. For part of what has been lost these past eight years can't just be measured by lost wages or bigger trade deficits. What has also been lost is our sense of common purpose—our sense of higher purpose. And that's what we have to restore.

We may not agree on abortion, but surely we can agree on reducing the number of unwanted pregnancies in this country. The reality of gun ownership may be different for hunters in rural Ohio than for those plagued by gang violence in Cleveland, but don't tell me we can't uphold the Second Amendment while keeping AK-47s out of the hands of criminals. I know there are differences on same-sex marriage, but surely we can agree that our gay and lesbian brothers and sisters deserve to visit the person they love in the hospital and to live lives free of discrimination. Passions fly on immigration, but I don't know anyone who benefits when a mother is separated from her infant child or an employer undercuts American wages by hiring illegal workers. This too is part of America's promise—the promise of a democracy where we can find the strength and grace to bridge divides and unite in common effort.

I know there are those who dismiss such beliefs as happy talk. They claim that our insistence on something larger, something firmer and more honest in our public life is just a Trojan horse for higher taxes and the abandonment of traditional values. And that's to be expected. Because if you don't have any fresh ideas, then you use stale tactics to scare the voters. If you don't have a record to run on, then you paint your opponent as someone people should run from.

You make a big election about small things.

And you know what—it's worked before. Because it feeds into the cynicism we all have about government. When Washington doesn't work, all its promises seem empty. If your hopes have been dashed again and again, then it's best to stop hoping, and settle for what you already know.

I get it. I realize that I am not the likeliest candidate for this office. I don't fit the typical pedigree, and I haven't spent my career in the halls of Washington. But I stand before you tonight because all across America something is stirring. What the naysayers don't understand is that this election has never been about me. It's been about you. For eighteen long months, you have stood up, one by one, and said "enough" to the politics of the past. You understand that in this election, the greatest risk we can take is to try the same old politics with the same old players and expect a different result. You have shown what history teaches us—that at defining moments like this one, the change we need doesn't come *from* Washington. Change comes *to* Washington. Change happens because the American people demand it—because they rise up and insist on new ideas and new leadership, a new politics for a new time.

America, this is one of those moments.

I believe that as hard as it will be, the change we need is coming. Because I've seen it. Because I've lived it. I've seen it in Illinois, when we provided health care to more children and moved more families from welfare to work. I've seen it in Washington, when we worked across party lines to open up government and hold lobbyists more accountable, to give better care for our veterans and keep nuclear weapons out of terrorist hands.

And I've seen it in this campaign. In the young people who voted for the first time, and in those who got involved again after a very long time. In the Republicans who never thought they'd pick up a Democratic ballot, but did. I've seen it in the workers who would rather cut their hours back a day than see their friends lose their jobs, in the soldiers who re-enlist after losing a limb, in the good neighbors who take a stranger in when a hurricane strikes and the floodwaters rise.

This country of ours has more wealth than any nation, but that's not what makes us rich. We have the most powerful military on Earth, but that's not what makes us strong. Our universities and our culture are the envy of the world, but that's not what keeps the world coming to our shores.

Instead, it is that American spirit—that American promise—that pushes us forward even when the path is uncertain, that binds us together in spite of our differences, that makes us fix our eye not on what is seen, but what is unseen, that better place around the bend.

That promise is our greatest inheritance. It's a promise I make to my daughters when I tuck them in at night, and a promise that you make to yours—a promise that has led immigrants to cross oceans and pioneers to travel west, a promise that led workers to picket lines, and women to reach for the ballot. And it is that promise that, forty five years ago today, brought Americans from every corner of this land to stand together on a Mall in Washington, before Lincoln's Memorial, and hear a young preacher from Georgia speak of his dream.

The men and women who gathered there could've heard many things. They could've heard words of anger and discord. They could've been told to succumb to the fear and frustration of so many dreams deferred. But what the people heard instead—people of every creed and color, from every walk of life—is that, in America, our destiny is inextricably linked. That, together, our dreams can be one.

"We cannot walk alone," the preacher cried.

"And as we walk, we must make the pledge that we shall always march ahead. We cannot turn back."

America, we cannot turn back. Not with so much work to be done. Not with so many children to educate, and so many veterans to care for. Not with an economy to fix and cities to rebuild and farms to save. Not with so many families to protect and so many lives to mend. America, we cannot turn back. We cannot walk alone. At this moment, in this election, we must pledge once more to march into the future. Let us keep that promise—that American promise—and in the words of Scripture hold firmly, without wavering, to the hope that we confess.

Thank you, God bless you, and God bless the United States of America.

WE CAN DO THIS
The Economic Crisis Speech
September 21, 2008

(Charlotte, North Carolina) Barack Obama delivered this campaign speech at a downtown rally, taking as his theme the economic crisis: *We can do this because Americans have done this before. Time and again, we've battled back from adversity by recognizing that common stake that we have in each other's success.*

The news of the day isn't good.

The era of greed and irresponsibility on Wall Street and in Washington has led us to a perilous moment. They said they wanted to let the market run free but instead they let it run wild. And now we are facing a financial crisis as profound as any we have faced since the Great Depression

But here's the truth—regardless of how we got here, we're here today. And the circumstances we face require decisive action because your jobs, your savings, and your economic security are now at risk.

We must work quickly in a bipartisan fashion to resolve this crisis to avert an even broader economic catastrophe. But Washington also has to recognize that economic recovery requires that we act, not just to address the crisis on Wall Street, but also the crisis on Main Street and around kitchen tables across America.

As of now, the Bush Administration has only offered a concept with a staggering price tag, not a plan. Even if the U.S. Treasury recovers some or most of its investment over time, this initial outlay of up to $700 billion is sobering. And, in return for their support, the American people must be assured that the deal reflects the basic principles of transparency, fairness, and reform.

First, there must be no blank check when American taxpayers are on the hook for this much money.

Second, taxpayers shouldn't be spending a dime to reward CEOs on Wall Street.

Third, taxpayers should be protected and should be able to recoup this investment.

Fourth, this plan has to help homeowners stay in their homes.

Fifth, this is a global crisis, and the United States must insist that other nations join us in helping secure the financial markets.

Sixth, we need to start putting in place the rules of the road I've been calling for for years to prevent this from ever happening again.

And finally, this plan can't just be a plan for Wall Street, it has to be a plan for Main Street. We have to come together, as Democrats and Republicans, to pass a stimulus plan that will put money in the pockets of working families, save jobs, and prevent painful budget cuts and tax hikes in our states.

So I know these are difficult days. But here's what I also know. I know we can steer ourselves out of this crisis. That's who we are. That's what we've always done as Americans. Our nation has faced difficult times before. And at each of those moments, we've risen to meet the challenge because we've never forgotten that fundamental truth—that here in America, our destiny is not written for us; it's written by us.

But another thing I know is this—we can't steer ourselves out of this crisis by heading in the same disastrous direction. And that's what this election is all about.

.... The radical idea that government has no role to play in protecting ordinary Americans has wreaked havoc on our economy....

What we've seen over the last few days is nothing less than the final verdict on this failed philosophy. And I am running for President of the United States because the dreams of the American people must not be endangered any more.

The times are too serious. The stakes are too high. At this moment, in this election, we need real change—change that's more than just a slogan, change that actually makes a difference in people's lives. And that's the kind of change I'll bring to Washington when I'm President of the United States of America.

That's the change the American people need.

Change means a tax code that doesn't reward the lobbyists who wrote it, but the American workers and small businesses who deserve it.... I will eliminate capital gains taxes for small businesses and start-ups—that's how we'll grow our economy and create the high-wage, high-tech jobs of tomorrow.

I will cut taxes—cut taxes—for 95% of all working families.... [In] an economy like this, the last thing we should do is raise taxes on the middle class.

I will finally keep the promise of affordable, accessible health care for every single American....

This is the change we need—the kind of bottom up growth and innovation that will advance the American economy by advancing the dreams of all Americans.

Times are hard. I will not pretend that the change we need will come without cost.... I know that we'll have to overcome our doubts and divisions and the determined opposition of powerful special interests before we can truly reform a broken economy and advance opportunity.

But I am running for President because we simply cannot afford four more years of an economic philosophy that works for Wall Street instead of Main Street, and ends up devastating both.

I don't want to wake up in four years to find that more Americans fell out of the middle class, and more families lost their savings. I don't want to see that our country failed to invest in our ability to compete, our children's future was mortgaged on another mountain of debt, and our financial markets failed to find a firmer footing.

At this defining moment, we have the chance to finally stand up and say—enough is enough!

We can do this because Americans have done this before. Time and again, we've battled back from adversity by recognizing that common stake that we have in each other's success. That's why our economy hasn't just been the world's greatest wealth generator—it's bound America together, it's created jobs, and it's made the dream of opportunity a reality for generation after generation of Americans.

Now it falls to us. And I need you to make it happen. If you want the next four years looking just like the last eight, then I am not your candidate. But if you want real change—if you want an economy that rewards work, and that works for Main Street *and*

Wall Street, if you want tax relief for the middle class and millions of new jobs, if you want health care you can afford and education that helps your kids compete—then I ask you to knock on some doors, make some calls, talk to your neighbors, and give me your vote on November 4th. And if you do, I promise you—we will win North Carolina, we will win this election, and we will change America together.

CHOOSING OUR BETTER HISTORY
The Time for Change Speech
October 29, 2008

(Sunrise, Florida) Barack Obama delivered this campaign speech at a rally at the BankAtlantic Center, taking as his theme the promise of change: *We can choose hope over fear, unity over division, the promise of change over the power of the status quo.... We can come together as one nation, and one people, and once more choose our better history.*

America, the time for change has come. And now, to all of those who've joined us from across this country, I say that in six days, we can choose an economy that rewards work and creates new jobs and fuels our prosperity, starting with the middle class.

In six days, we can choose to invest in health care for our families, and education for our kids, and renewable energy for our future.

In six days, we can choose hope over fear, unity over division, the promise of change over the power of the status quo.

In six days, we can come together as one nation, and one people, and once more choose our better history.

That's what's at stake. That's what we're fighting for—for the small business owner in Denver to keep his doors open, for the hardworking couple in Cincinnati to retire in comfort, for the young student in Ft. Lauderdale to afford her tuition, for men and women in every city and town across this nation to achieve the American Dream.

And if in this last week, you will knock on some doors for me, and make some calls for me, and go to barackobama.com and find out where to vote, if you will stand with me, and fight by my side, and cast your ballot for me, then I promise you this—we will not just win Florida, we will not just win this election but, together, we will change this country and we will change the world.

Thank you, God bless you, and may God bless America.

YES, WE CAN!
The Victory Speech
November 4, 2008

(Chicago, Illinois) Barack Obama delivered this victory speech before a crowd of hundreds of thousands at Grant Park: *This is our time ... to reclaim the American dream and reaffirm that fundamental truth that, out of many, we are one, that while we breathe, we hope. And where we are met with cynicism and doubts and those who tell us that we can't, we will respond with that timeless creed that sums up the spirit of a people—Yes, we can!*

If there is anyone out there who still doubts that America is a place where all things are possible, who still wonders if the dream of our founders is alive in our time, who still questions the power of our democracy, tonight is your answer.

It's the answer told by lines that stretched around schools and churches in numbers this nation has never seen, by people who waited three hours and four hours, many for the first time in their lives, because they believed that this time must be different, that their voices could be that difference.

It's the answer spoken by young and old, rich and poor, Democrat and Republican, black, white, Hispanic, Asian, Native American, gay, straight, disabled, and not disabled. Americans who sent a message to the world that we have never been just a collection of individuals or a collection of red states and blue states.

We are, and always will be, the United States of America.

It's the answer that led those who've been told for so long by so many to be cynical and fearful and doubtful about what we can achieve to put their hands on the arc of history and bend it once more toward the hope of a better day.

It's been a long time coming but, tonight, because of what we did on this date in this election at this defining moment change has come to America.

.... [Above] all, I will never forget who this victory truly belongs to. It belongs to you. It belongs to you.

I was never the likeliest candidate for this office. We didn't start with much money or many endorsements. Our campaign was not hatched in the halls of Washington. It began in the backyards of Des Moines and the living rooms of Concord and the front porches of Charleston. It was built by working men and women who dug into what little savings they had to give $5 and $10 and $20 to the cause.

It grew strength from the young people who rejected the myth of their generation's apathy—who left their homes and their families for jobs that offered little pay and less sleep.

It drew strength from the not-so-young people who braved the bitter cold and scorching heat to knock on doors of perfect strangers, and from the millions of Americans who volunteered and organized and proved that, more than two centuries later, a government of the people, by the people, and for the people, has not perished from the Earth.

This is your victory. And I know you didn't do this just to win an election. And I know you didn't do it for me. You did it because you understand the enormity of the task that lies ahead. For even as we celebrate tonight, we know the challenges that tomorrow will bring are the greatest of our lifetime—two wars, a planet in peril, the worst financial crisis in a century.

Even as we stand here tonight, we know there are brave Americans waking up in the deserts of Iraq and the mountains of Afghanistan to risk their lives for us.

There are mothers and fathers who will lie awake after the children fall asleep and wonder how they'll make the mortgage or pay their doctors' bills or save enough for their child's college education.

There's new energy to harness, new jobs to be created, new schools to build, and threats to meet, alliances to repair.

The road ahead will be long. Our climb will be steep. We may not get there in one year or even in one term. But, America, I have never been more hopeful than I am tonight that we will get there.

I promise you, we as a people will get there.

There will be setbacks and false starts. There are many who won't agree with every decision or policy I make as president. And we know the government can't solve every problem.

But I will always be honest with you about the challenges we face. I will listen to you—especially when we disagree. And, above all, I will ask you to join in the work of remaking this nation—the only way it's been done in America for 221 years—block by block, brick by brick, calloused hand by calloused hand.

What began 21 months ago in the depths of winter cannot end on this autumn night. This victory alone is not the change we seek. It is only the chance for us to make that change. And that cannot happen if we go back to the way things were.

It can't happen without you, without a new spirit of service, a new spirit of sacrifice. So let us summon a new spirit of patriotism, of responsibility—where each of us resolves to pitch in and work harder and look after not only ourselves but each other.

Let us remember that, if this financial crisis taught us anything, it's that we cannot have a thriving Wall Street while Main Street suffers.

In this country, we rise or fall as one nation, as one people. Let's resist the temptation to fall back on the same partisanship and pettiness and immaturity that has poisoned our politics for so long. Let's remember that it was a man from this state who first carried the banner of the Republican Party to the White House, a party founded on the values of self-reliance and individual liberty and national unity. Those are values that we all share. And while the Democratic Party has won a great victory tonight, we do so with a measure of humility and determination to heal the divides that have held back our progress.

As Lincoln said to a nation far more divided than ours, we are not enemies but friends. Though passion may have strained, it must not break our bonds of affection. And to those Americans whose support I have yet to earn, I may not have won your vote tonight, but I hear your voices. I need your help. And I will be your president too.

And to all those watching tonight from beyond our shores—from parliaments and palaces, to those who are huddled around radios in the forgotten corners of the world—our stories are singular, but our destiny is shared, and a new dawn of American leadership is at hand.

To those … who would tear the world down—we will defeat you. To those who seek peace and security—we support you. And to all those who have wondered if America's beacon still burns as bright—tonight we proved once more that the true strength of our nation comes not from the might of our arms or the scale of our wealth, but from the enduring power of our ideals—democracy, liberty, opportunity, and unyielding hope.

That's the true genius of America—that America can change. Our union can be perfected. What we've already achieved gives us hope for what we can and must achieve tomorrow.

This election had many firsts and many stories that will be told for generations. But one that's on my mind tonight's about a woman who cast her ballot in Atlanta. She's a lot like the millions of others who stood in line to make their voice heard in this election, except for one thing—Ann Nixon Cooper is 106 years old.

She was born just a generation past slavery—a time when there were no cars on the road or planes in the sky, when someone like her couldn't vote for two reasons—because she was a woman, and because of the color of her skin.

And tonight, I think about all that she's seen throughout her century in America—the heartache and the hope, the struggle and the progress, the times we were told that we can't, and the people who pressed on with that American creed—Yes, we can!

At a time when women's voices were silenced and their hopes dismissed, she lived to see them stand up and speak out and reach for the ballot. Yes, we can!

When there was despair in the dust bowl and depression across the land, she saw a nation conquer fear itself with a New Deal, new jobs, a new sense of common purpose. Yes, we can!

When the bombs fell on our harbor and tyranny threatened the world, she was there to witness a generation rise to greatness and a democracy was saved. Yes, we can!

She was there for the buses in Montgomery, the hoses in Birmingham, a bridge in Selma, and a preacher from Atlanta who told a people that *We Shall Overcome*. Yes, we can!

A man touched down on the moon, a wall came down in Berlin, a world was connected by our own science and imagination. And this year, in this election, she touched her finger to a screen, and cast her vote, because after 106 years in America, through the best of times and the darkest of hours, she knows how America can change.

Yes, we can!

America, we have come so far. We have seen so much. But there is so much more to do. So tonight, let us ask ourselves—if our children should live to see the next century, if my daughters should be so lucky to live as long as Ann Nixon Cooper, what change will they see? What progress will we have made?

This is our chance to answer that call. This is our moment.

This is our time—to put our people back to work and open doors of opportunity for our kids, to restore prosperity and promote the cause of peace, to reclaim the American dream and reaffirm that fundamental truth that, out of many, we are one, that while we breathe, we hope.

And, where we are met with cynicism and doubts and those who tell us that we can't, we will respond with that timeless creed that sums up the spirit of a people—Yes, we can!

Thank you. God bless you. And may God bless the United States of America.

BIBLIOGRAPHY

Ahuja, Sunil, and Robert Dewhirst, Editors. *The Road to Congress 2004*. New York, NY: Nova Science Publishers, 2005.

Barkley, Charles. *Who's Afraid of a Large Black Man?* New York, NY: Penguin Press, 2005.

Brill, Marlene Targ. *Barack Obama: Working to Make a Difference*. Brookfield, CT: Millbrook Press, 2006.

Daley, James. *Great Speeches by African Americans: Frederick Douglass, Sojourner Truth, Dr. Martin Luther King, Jr., Barack Obama, and Others*. Mineola, NY: Dover Publications, 2006.

Devaney, Sherri, and Mark Devaney. *Barack Obama*. San Diego, CA: Lucent Books, 2006.

Dupuis, Martin, and Keith Boeckelman. *Barack Obama: The New Face of American Politics*. Westport, CT: Praeger, 2008.

Falsani, Cathleen. *The God Factor: Inside the Spiritual Lives of Public People*. New York, NY: Farrar, Straus & Giroux, 2006.

Hazen, Don, and Lakshmi Chaudhry, Editors. *Start Making Sense: Turning the Elections of 2004 into Winning Progressive Politics*. White River Junction, VT: Chelsea Green Publishing Co., 2005.

Mendell, David. *Obama: From Promise to Power*. New York, NY: Amistad/Harper Collins Publishers, 2007.

Obama, Barack. *The Audacity of Hope: Thoughts on Reclaiming the American Dream*. New York, NY: Crown Books, 2006.

___. *Dreams From My Father: A Story of Race and Inheritance*. New York, NY: Crown Books, 2007.

Rogak, Lisa, Editor. *Barack Obama In His Own Words*. New York, NY: Carroll & Graf, 2004.

📖 EXCELLENT BOOKS ORDER FORM 📖
(Please xerox this form so it will be available to other readers.)

Please send the following books:
___ Barack Obama: Speeches On The Road To The White House
___ The Speeches of Abraham Lincoln
___ The Speeches of Ronald Reagan
___ Landmark Decisions of the U.S. Supreme Court I
___ Landmark Decisions of the U.S. Supreme Court II
___ Landmark Decisions of the U.S. Supreme Court III
___ Landmark Decisions of the U.S. Supreme Court IV
___ Landmark Decisions of the U.S. Supreme Court V
___ Landmark Decisions of the U.S. Supreme Court VI
___ Landmark Decisions of the U.S. Supreme Court VII
___ Freedom of Speech Decisions
___ Freedom of the Press Decisions

All Excellent Books are $24.95 each.
Order directly from us for a discount.
Add $2.00 shipping/handling for the first book
and $1.00 each for every other book ordered.

Name: _____

Organization: _____

Address: _____

E-mail: _____ Fax: _____

City: _____ State: _____ Zip: _____

Send your check or purchase order to:
Excellent Books, POB 131322, Carlsbad, CA 92013-1322
Phone: **760-598-5069**; Fax: **240-218-7601**
E-mail: **books@excellentbooks.com**
or visit our website at **excellentbooks.com**